Tr... guide
to the
South of France

MAURICE ROSENBAUM

GEOGRAPHIA

Other titles in this series are:

Travellers' Guide to Egypt
Travellers' Guide to Portugal
Travellers' Guide to Greece
Travellers' Guide to Ireland
Travellers' Guide to Israel
Travellers' Guide to Malta, Gozo and Comino
Travellers' Guide to Southern Africa

Thornton Cox Travellers' Guides
South of France
© Geographia Limited 1983
First published 1975
New Edition 1983

Text by Maurice Rosenbaum
Additional material by Geographia Limited
Maps by Tom Stalker-Miller, M.S.I.A.
Drawings by Guy Magnus

Photographs by courtesy of the French Government
Tourist Office

Geographia Limited
17–21 Conway Street
London W1P 6JD

Set in Univers by Rowland Phototypesetting Ltd,
Bury St Edmunds, Suffolk

Colour separations by Dot Gradations Ltd, Chelmsford, Essex
Colour plates printed by George Over Ltd, Rugby
Printed and bound by The Guernsey Press Co Ltd,
Guernsey, Channel Islands

ISBN 0 09 207910 5

Les antiques St-Rémy de Provence

Contents

Acknowledgements

The publishers would like to thank the French Government Tourist Office for their facilities and assistance during research work for this book.

Foreword

The holiday attractions of the South of France are almost infinite; more than enough to appeal to most tastes in relaxation – physical exercise, exploration, sunbathing, or simply watching life in an unfamiliar setting flow round you in the morning sun.

It is a country made for such enjoyment, with outdoor café-terraces, village squares, great tracts of herb-scented *garrigue* or moorland, and mountains with almost impenetrable undergrowth and woodland – the *maquis* – to visit and explore. There are also ski-resorts within very convenient reach.

Then there are, of course, the so well-known delights of southern France: the food and wine, the shops and antiquities, the breathtaking survivors from a chequered past such as Carcassonne, or the Château de Salses, or the beautiful abbeys of the Pyrenees. Start with a conducted tour, by all means, to whet your appetite. Then go it alone and at leisure.

Obviously, you'll get more out of your holiday in the *Midi* if you know some French: for one thing, you'll be able to explore farther under your own steam and so discover out-of-the-way places and people who will go to endless trouble to show you the best of their own region. But a little French goes a long way, and you don't need an extensive vocabulary to explore the countryside within reach of your base, or to sit in a village café with a glass of wine or *pastis*, or to wander round the old towns on foot with a street map.

Inland from the sun-baked beaches many villages are to be found perched in the hills and mountains: these hill-top villages are typical of Provence and, indeed, of the whole of the South. Some have already been prettified or transformed into a collection of tourist-trap boutiques, but many of them – many more than the unadventurous traveller may realise – are still unspoilt. They differ considerably in colour, character and remoteness, from the red sandstone, ochre and pantile clusters of the Languedoc and Roussillon, west of the Rhône valley, to the golden-grey fastnesses perched higher and more strongly-walled in the hills to the east, near the Italian frontier.

In these villages are to be found those elements which entice the northern city-dweller: sun-warmed stone and plane-tree shade, olive groves, lemons, mimosa and oleanders, bougainvillea and lizards on low walls, small shops and street markets – not to mention the best climate in Europe.

They have, too, easy access to that marvellous coast and sea which, in the gaps between the busy resorts, is still one of the best holiday areas in the world. Don't make the mistake of writing off the Côte d'Azur and the Riviera because of what you have heard of the effects of package tours, over-building or pollution. Package tours give opportunities to get there cheaply and nobody is compelled to stay in a crowd. Pollution is, of course, a real problem, here as almost everywhere else in the seas of the world (nuclear and oil waste even where there is no serious quantity of human sewage), and the problem will have to be tackled before it is too late. But there are still stretches of unpolluted beach and sea between Marseilles and Menton (and even more between Marseilles and the Spanish frontier). Don't, therefore, allow yourself to miss any opportunity of seeing the colour and grandeur of the Esterel, the classical pine-clad coast of the Maures, and the lovely wooded capes and islands off the coast between Hyères and Menton.

The role played by the Mediterranean countries in world history must surely have some part in every European and American consciousness, however little detailed history the traveller may have read. The past is certainly all around in the presence of the people, whose physique, looks and local dialects reflect their links with the ancient world of Greece and Rome, the Arab empires and the Northern invaders. The historical flashbacks given in this book will, I hope, help to illuminate the walls of a castle or the alleyways of an old town for those whose knowledge of this or that dynasty, migration, battle, invasion or settlement is somewhat less than the learned scholar's.

What follows is, necessarily, a selection from the many places and resources of the South of France. I hope it will encourage travellers to make their own exploration and discoveries.

General Information

Getting There

The South of France offers infinite scope for the independent traveller, whilst those who prefer to take an 'off the peg' holiday are well catered for by a variety of reliable tour operators. And planning your travel arrangements is certainly part of the fun of visiting this region.

By Air

The quickest route is, of course, by air; from London to Nice takes just under two hours and British Airways and Air France operate direct flights daily. Nice Airport, tel. (93) 83 03 00 (Air Inter), handles flights to and from numerous international destinations, including a daily direct service from New York. Marseilles Airport, tel. (91) 91 90 90 also operates internationally; both British Airways and Air France fly direct. Air France also make regular flights from London to Toulouse, tel. (61) 62 59 52.

The South of France is well served by airports and in addition to those already mentioned you can fly to Perpignan, tel. (68) 61 22 24, Montpellier, tel. (67) 58 26 80, Nimes, tel. (66) 20 12 40 and Toulon, tel. (94) 57 41 41, but normally only by transferring at Paris to pick up an Air Inter flight. Air Inter, the French internal airline system, operates an extensive network of routes throughout France and all airports serving the South have direct flights to Paris from where you can fly to almost any corner of the globe.

Flying is expensive, but shop around to get the best deal: the regular return air fare from London to Nice is around £296, while it is possible to get a Fly-Drive package with Dan Air for under £200. For further information about flying to the South of France contact Air France at 158 New Bond Street, London W1Y 0AY, British Airways at 75 Regent Street, London SW1 (for reservations ring (01) 370 5411) or the French Tourist Office at 178 Piccadilly, London W1V 0AL, tel. (01) 491 7622, which will provide excellent information on all aspects of visiting France. In the U.S.A. the French Government Tourist Office is located at 610 5th Avenue, New York NY 10020; tel. (212) 757 1125, and in Canada at 372 Bay Street, Suite 610, Toronto M5H 2W9; tel. (416) 361 1605.

Internal Flights

Air Inter offers worthwhile reductions on many flights, including international flights incorporating an Air Inter leg, as well as further reductions for students, young people under 25, pensioners, families (minimum three) and groups of ten or more – for full details write to Air Inter, Foreign Dept., 8 rue Gauguet, 75014 Paris.

Fly-Drive

Dan Air, Croydon, tel. (01) 680 1011, operates services from Aberdeen to

Toulouse, Gatwick to Perpignan, Montpellier and Toulouse and from New-castle to Toulouse. It is well worth investigating the Fly-Drive fares Dan Air offers in conjunction with Hertz which ensure the availability of a car on arrival and represent considerable savings on separate arrangements.

By Car
If time is not of the essence then a far more pleasurable way of getting to the South of France from the U.K. is by car. The most direct route is on the fast motorway (designated A – *autoroute*) via Paris (A 26, A 1), Lyon (A 6) and Avignon (A 7), but there are many alternative and more scenic routes using either the national roads (designated N – *nationale*) or secondary roads (designated D – *départementale*) including the traditional central route via Paris, Moulins, Lyon and thence south following the autoroute – but without paying the rather expensive tolls (toll routes are clearly marked *péage*). If you are heading south west, then it is worth considering travelling via Rouen (avoiding Paris), Chartres, Orleans, Limoges and Cahors. Allow two days or more for the trip by car.

Before starting your journey a good road map is always a wise investment allowing you to plan the journey carefully in advance. Geographia and Michelin publish good maps covering the whole of France, and whilst buying your route-planning map consideration should be given to the more detailed local maps you will need as well. Geographia produce good regional maps of South East and South West France and for more detail still the I.G.N. (the French equivalent of Ordnance Survey maps) *Cartes Touristiques* 1:250,000, the Michelin 1:200,000 series and the Recta Foldex regional maps at 1:250,000, are excellent touring aids.

When travelling by car remember that you will need a current driving licence (minimum age 18), the vehicle registration book, international third party insurance, but preferably comprehensive and signified by a green card, a GB or nationality sticker and a red triangle in case of breakdown. Drive on the right and give priority to traffic coming from the right (*priorité à droite*). And remember to adjust your headlights for driving on the right; the French are accustomed to amber headlights and there is nothing more annoying to the French driver than to be dazzled by white, unadjusted lights! Two grades of petrol are normally available, *super* – high octane (4 star) and *normale* (2 star). Speed limits in force are 60 kph in built-up areas, 90 kph on *routes nationales* and 130 kph on the *autoroutes*. Wear seat belts if fitted and observe the rules – police who patrol roads and motorways (Garde Mobile) have powers to fine offenders on the spot. The choice of route through France will tend to determine where you cross the channel. The English Channel, apart from being the most crowded shipping route in the world, is also the most competitive – there are numerous crossing points and six major companies operating services:–

Brittany Ferries:	Portsmouth – St. Malo Plymouth – Roscoff
Hoverspeed:	Dover – Calais and Boulogne Ramsgate – Calais
P & O Ferries:	Dover – Boulogne Southampton – Le Havre

Sally – The Viking Line:	Ramsgate – Dunkerque
Sealink:	Dover – Dunkerque, Calais and Boulogne
	Folkestone – Calais
	Newhaven – Dieppe
	Weymouth – Cherbourg
Townsend–Thoresen:	Dover – Calais
	Portsmouth – Le Havre and Cherbourg
	Southampton – Le Havre and Cherbourg

If you plan to take one of the westerly routes through France a crossing to St Malo, Cherbourg, Le Havre or Dieppe could save you time. By hovercraft France is just 40 minutes away with easy disembarkation on arrival. Tariffs resemble a jungle and vary with crossing, season, length of vehicle and so forth, although stiff competition for business has helped to hold fares at reasonable levels and off-peak and low season rates are available. Sally – The Viking Line, a relative newcomer to the cross-channel business, offers a simple tariff and attractive fares – a high season return crossing inclusive of car (any size) and two adults costs around £80, and up to two children under 14 travel free.

By Coach

An increasingly popular and economical way of travelling to the South of France is by one of the regular coach services operating from London and selected points. Euroways, 7 York Way, London N1 9UD, tel. (01) 278 0831, operates from London and Dover to Antibes, Cannes, Lyon, Marseilles, Montpellier and Nice.

By Train

'Let the train take the strain' is a particularly useful idea if you are looking for a fast, pleasurable way to the South of France at prices to compete with the cheapest air fares. The train journey from London (Victoria) to Nice takes about 20 hours and there are some excellent trains plying the route with couchette, sleeper and restaurant services (for example the luxury day train, the *Mistral* and the *Train Bleu* which makes the journey overnight). Fast trains run from Paris to Toulouse, Montpellier and Marseilles and there is a comprehensive network of routes allowing access to most parts of the South by train. For the rail enthusiast there is the exhilarating 162 mph T.G.V. (*Train à Grande Vitesse*) running from Paris to Lyon in just two hrs 40 mins.

Attractive fare bargains are available on French Railways, including a Holiday Return (*Séjour*) Ticket which allows a 25 percent reduction on the ordinary fare for return journeys of over 1000 km, Party Tickets giving a 20 percent reduction for ten adults or more, the *France Vacances* card providing unlimited travel throughout the network at very reasonable rates and the *Carte Vermeil* for senior citizens with a reduction of 50 percent on the basic fare. For the under 26s an Inter-rail ticket costing just over £100 entitles the holder to half price travel in the U.K. plus unlimited free travel in any of the 19 countries, including France, participating in the scheme.

Motorail

If you want your car in the South of France without the stress of driving it there then use the French Motorail service; put the car on the train at Calais or Boulogne for one of the Motorail terminals at Avignon, Narbonne, Nice or St-Raphaël – and relax. Alternatively you can pick up the Motorail service at Paris for these and other destinations. Fast and comfortable with a variety of good sleeping accommodation, but it's not cheap and you may miss some of the pleasant watering holes to be discovered on the drive down. For further information on travelling by rail consult your travel agent or French Railways Ltd., 179 Piccadilly, London W1V 0BA; tel. (01) 493 9731.

It is readily apparent from this brief survey that there are many ways of getting to the South of France, and in addition to making your own arrangements, there is a great variety of inclusive tours available, incorporating any combination of travel and accommodation, which any good travel agent will be able to advise you on. The French Tourist Office in London issues a useful booklet providing names and addresses of companies specialising in French holidays and travel.

Car Hire

Car hire is normally no problem in the South of France; there are agencies in all large towns; Hertz, Avis, Budget and Europ Car are also located at most airports. There are numerous local hire companies offering competitive rates, but for peace of mind it is sensible to go for one of the known international companies. Check age limits – normally you need to be over 21 (in some cases over 23) and under 65 to hire a car. You must have a current driving licence held for at least one year. For a small car, eg Renault 5, the daily rate is around £12 plus a small charge per kilometre. Weekly rates are more advantageous. Third Party insurance is usually included although it is well worth taking out full cover for a small additional fee. There is normally a deposit to find, although holders of major credit cards are exempt.

Public Transport

Public transport in the South of France is generally excellent. There are good train services connecting the principal towns; trains tend to run north-south and along the Mediterranean coast and in the high season are a sensible alternative to using the frequently overcrowded roads. Both private and public bus services will get you to most destinations and local tourist offices or *Syndicats d'Initiative* (referred to in the text either in full or abbreviated to S.I.) will supply routes and timetables on request. Scenic tours are available from terminals in Nice, Marseilles, Toulouse and most major tourist centres.

Accommodation

From luxury hotels to small tents, a very wide range of accommodation is now available for the visitor to the South of France. Hotels are graded from one to four stars plus a luxury category; you will not always find the word *hotel* in the name, but *relais*, *residence*, *auberge* and *pension* are all equivalents, the latter being more like the English guest house. You normally pay for a double room without meals and a comfortable but modest hotel will cost around £12 a night, but will vary considerably depending on whether you stay at one of the popular coastal resorts or inland off the beaten track where living is still good and cheap. On the whole, hotels in the South of France represent very good value for money, and if the hotel has a restaurant it's usually worth trying out.

Self-catering is becoming increasingly popular in the region; villas, flats and houses are offered for rent either direct or more usually through tour or villa companies. If self-catering without the constraints of a package tour appeals, then the growing selection of *Gîtes de France* is worth looking into – these are privately owned rural holiday homes partly financed by the French government. Weekly rates for four to six people average around £75 and full information may be obtained from Gîtes de France, 178 Piccadilly, London W1V 0PQ.

Caravanning and Camping

For the past decade or more the South of France has been successfully invaded by campers and caravanners but more recently the business of hiring out caravans or tents on site as part of an inclusive package has come to the fore. However you arrange things a good site is essential. In France caravan and camp sites are graded from one to four stars depending on amenities, size of plots and the efficiency of site management. There is an enormous choice, so unless you enjoy crowds and noise it's best to avoid the very large sites where campers exist like sardines in depressing, if usually clean and efficient uniformity. Some of the smaller sites, usually away from the coast, can be a delightful experience. Michelin and Letts publish guides to sites in France and, for the Mediterranean coast only, Roger Lascelles' guide lists over 120 useful sites. But bear in mind that experience counts for a lot when it comes to camping and caravanning, so if in doubt talk to someone who has done it!

A note of caution: the French pride themselves on the high standard of their camping sites and on the way they are sited. But these accredited sites are in great demand and it is essential, for the peak holiday periods, to make reservations in advance through the camping agencies, details of which can be obtained from the French Government Tourist Office at 178 Piccadilly, London W1V 0AL. In some areas the behaviour of tourists who arrive without having booked places on sites is giving concern to the French authorities, both national and regional. Visitors who pitch tents wherever they find themselves, with disregard for local amenities or simple hygiene – and without seeking permission – make things difficult for all other campers.

More information from the A.A. and R.A.C. The Caravan Club Ltd., East Grinstead House, East Grinstead, West Sussex RH19 1UA; tel. (0342) 311 844, runs a Foreign Touring Services department and campers should look at services offered by the Camping Club of Great Britain, 11 Lower Grosvenor Place, London SW1 W0EY; tel. (01) 828 1012.

Medical Care

Health matters deserve attention when planning your trip. Fortunately, hospitals and medical care in the South of France are of a high standard and visitors from E.E.C. countries are normally covered under the French social security system which provides free hospital treatment and refunds about 80 percent of a G.P.'s costs (you will have to wait a day or so for the refund whilst formalities are completed). However, it is generally wise to take out separate full medical cover for a worry-free trip. Should you require medical attention at any time it is best to start with the hotel reception which will normally put you in touch with a doctor. For minor ailments chemists (*pharmacie*), indicated by a green cross, are very helpful; the French pharmacist is trained more like a doctor for consultation on minor ills. *Pharmacies a garde*, or duty chemists, are listed in the local paper and their names and addresses are available from a police station or tourist office.

U.K. citizens can obtain full details of free medical protection in France in booklet SA 30 available from any social security office; you will need to complete form CM 1 and will be given form E 111 to take with you as evidence of entitlement to free medical treatment.

Tap water in the South of France is quite safe (except, of course when marked '*eau non potable*' – not drinking water) even though mineral water might be the preferable drink; stomach upsets are normally caused by too much sun and an unaccustomed, often rich, diet – so start off with both in moderation.

Currency and Banking

Opinion is divided on whether it is best to take French currency, English travellers cheques or travellers cheques in French currency. For most holiday purposes a combination of currency and travellers cheques is advisable and if you purchase cheques in francs they tend to be easier to cash in smaller banks and other establishments and you will not be faced with the ups and downs in rates of exchange.

The prime unit of French currency is the *franc* F, divided into 100 *centimes*: coins include 10, 20 and 50 centimes and notes 10, 20, 50, 100 and 500 francs. Like £.s.d. in the U.K., old monetary systems die hard so that people in France still sometimes refer to 'old francs' which disappeared over 20 years ago – 100 old francs = 1 new franc.

Banks open 09.00–12.00 and 14.00–16.00 weekdays and are usually closed on Saturdays (sometimes Mondays). If you need to change money, make for a bank rather than a *bureau de change* where the rate tends to be lower; a hotel will often oblige but the rate of exchange will not be favourable. With a eurocheque encashment card, available on application from most English banks, you can cash two cheques a day up to £50 each. The Midland Bank issues its own eurocheques and eurocards, with which larger amounts of money can be cashed, but in the smaller towns and villages of the South changing foreign money in any form can still pose problems, so be prepared.

American Express, Visa (*Carte Bleue*) and Diners Club cards are accepted in most major hotels, restaurants and shops, especially along the Côte d'Azur, but in general you will not find it standard practice for the southern French to trade with plastic as it is in many other areas of Europe and the U.S.A. in particular.

Climate

Allowing for variations in weather where hills and mountains cause sharper winters and higher rainfall, the South of France enjoys one of the pleasantest climates in Europe with scorching summers and mild, dry winters. West of Toulon the coastal areas are affected by the *mistral* wind blowing down the Rhône valley and the *tramontane* from the Pyrénées; the *mistral* is particularly aggressive in March but can rise quite suddenly at any time, even in summer.

In July and August the region is at its hottest (temperatures can often stay at 30°C around the clock) and the most crowded, although in the Roussillon and Languedoc the weather is a little less predictable than on the Côte d'Azur. Spring and Autumn are the rainy seasons, but the short, heavy showers are quickly replaced by idyllic spells of warm sunshine when the wild flowers and lush vegetation may be seen at their best. The average temperature at these times of the year is 17°C. Winters in the coastal South are usually mild (the temperature rarely falls below 10°C) and rainfall is slight, and it is no accident that the Riviera at this time of year became the refuge of Europe's aristocracy and royalty as early as the 18th century.

Throughout the South of France the quality of the light is remarkable; bright and luminescent, in combination with the richness and colours of the land-scape it is prized by artists and visitors alike.

For wildlife and nature enthusiasts the region has much to offer, especially in the area at the mouth of the Rhône known as the *Camargue*. Lemon, orange, fig and olive trees, as well as a rich variety of wild herbs and flowers, thrive along the Mediterranean coast whilst the hinterland gives way to forests of pine and beech, vast areas of dry scrub (the *maquis*), fertile valleys with vine-clad slopes and snow-capped mountains. In short, it is an area of contrasts full of never-ending delights for the visitor.

Customs

A valid passport is essential. Visas are not normally required and there are no health requirements for visitors from the U.K., Europe and North America. There are generous duty-free allowances on such items as cigarettes, wines and spirits and perfumes being brought into France, but check since these change from time to time and vary slightly between imports from E.E.C. countries and other parts of the world; it's essential for U.K. visitors to know what restrictions apply for re-entry as the customs control on the return trip is likely to be more rigorous. Both countries are particularly vigilant against the transportation and use of drugs. Whilst there is no limit on the importation of foreign currency or travellers cheques, you are not permitted to take out of the country more than 5000F in French currency.

Food

The South of France might well be described as a gourmet's melting pot; although Provençale cooking is the predominant influence, Italian and Spanish dishes have blended successfully with the local cuisine to add great variety to menus throughout the region. Don't expect to find too much in the way of French classical cuisine, although it is served in some of the major restaurants and hotels.

The hallmarks of Provençale cookery are goodly quantities of garlic, olive oil, herbs, onions and tomatoes – although not always in that order and not as overpowering as the list might suggest: in fact, dishes *à la Provençale* can often be subtle as well as exceptionally tasty. Soups are excellent – but usually filling. Try the local fish soup, *soupe de poissons*, made from finely ground small fish, garnished with grated cheese and served with *rouille* (a red sauce of Spanish peppers and garlic). *Soupe au Pistou* is a thick vegetable soup topped with cheese and very satisfying.

The South of France is a paradise for lovers of fish, with plenty of fresh water and sea varieties available. Particularly good and not too expensive are the *dorade* (sea bream), *loup de mer* (sea bass) and *rouget* (red mullet). Shell fish are usually imported. Lobster (*langouste* – *langoustine* is a smaller, but equally delicious type) is expensive everywhere, but mediterranean prawns make a tasty and cheaper alternative. Many other fish delicacies abound in the small ports along the coast, where you can find mussels (*moules*) cooked in white wine, sea anemones (*violets*), Rhône eels and octopus. But the king of fish dishes in the South is surely the *bouillabaisse*, a fish stew crammed with an assortment of fish and shell fish; every town and restaurant has its own particular version, although Marseilles claims to be the place to eat it. But be warned, although undoubtedly an adventure worth the experience, *bouillabaisse* is a big meal requiring both appetite and patience!

Meat and poultry are plentiful and frequently appetizingly prepared on charcoal grills or spit-roasts. Beef from the Camargue, often dubbed *boeuf gardien*, is worth keeping an eye open for. *Daubes* – or stews – are a feature of the region, served with noodles topped with sauce from the stockpot (*macaronade*). For the more adventurous there is *pieds et paquets*, a traditional Provençale dish of sheep's tripe stuffed with the trotters, pork, garlic and onions and simmered long in white wine, or *alouettes sans têtes*, tender veal stuffed with cured ham, pork and herbs. *Saucissons* and sausages from Arles and Toulouse tend to have the edge on their British counterparts.

The southern climate favours the cultivation of superb vegetables and fruit; melons, peaches, apricots, grapes and figs are plentiful and the enormous variety of vegetable dishes is an attractive feature of the cuisine. *Ratatouille* is a popular speciality made from a combination of tomatoes, onions, aubergines, courgettes and green peppers cooked in oil and, as a first course or light main meal, *Salade Niçoise*, which includes black olives, hard-boiled egg and tuna fish makes an appetising dish. And the *assiette de crudités* or raw vegetable salad is always reliable – try it with *aïoli*, a garlic-flavoured mayonnaise used as a dip. All sorts of snacks are popular with tourists and locals alike, including pizzas, *socca* (a kind of pancake from Nice), *tourtes* (savoury vegetable pastries) and *tian* (vegetable omelette); but remember that sandwiches are larger than life and made of long sections of French bread – *pain bagnats*, bread buns filled with fresh tomatoes, sliced onions, hard-boiled eggs and anchovies, are a tasty, lighter alternative, especially on the beach.

Don't neglect the tempting variety of rough country pâtés and the local cheeses, especially the drier ones made from goats or sheeps milk (*de chèvres* or *de brebis*).

Wines
It is often the case that regional wines tend to complement the local food and the South of France is no exception: the southern French wines are generally

light, dry and refreshing and you will be hard-put to find a better accompaniment to the cuisine. Unfortunately, in the past the wines of the South have been overshadowed by the grander vintages of Bordeaux, Bourgogne and Beaujolais. But as these have become more and more expensive, growers in the South have put more energy into cultivating and expanding the vineyards of Provence, Languedoc-Roussillon and the Côtes du Rhône with encouraging results.

The whites are generally dry and go well with local seafood dishes – *Cassis* and *Palette* are notable whites. Rosé wines from Provence and Tavel served chilled are light, refreshing and relatively cheap. Red wines are however more abundant and amongst them some excellent varieties are to be found: from Languedoc-Roussillon come *Muscat, Minervois, Corbierres, Fitou* and *Côtes du Roussillon.* The best Provençale reds are *Bandol* and *Palette,* and the Rhône wines are numerous and good, although a little more expensive. *Chateauneuf-du-Pape* with its mellow, faintly aromatic taste is the most famous of the Rhône wines, but others from areas such as *Gigondas* and *Lirac* are well worth trying.

Festivals

The South of France is rich in musical, religious, cultural and sporting events throughout the year; the Monte Carlo Rally (January), Nice Carnival (February), the Battle of Flowers at Vence (April), the Cannes Film Festival, Monaco Grand Prix and Grasse Rose Festival (May), Festival of Sacred Music in Nice (June), the music festivals at Aix-en-Provence and Monaco (July and August) and the Menton International Chamber Music Festival are only the tip of the iceberg. For comprehensive information on all cultural events, there is a useful guide entitled *Festivals in France* available from French Tourist Offices.

Gratuities

Tipping has always been a potential source of embarrassment to the Anglo-Saxon visitor to mediterranean countries, but if you remember a few simple rules you should find no problem in the South of France. Tipping for any service received is a way of life but no-one is going to get too ruffled if a visitor doesn't get it quite right. Restaurants and hotels normally add a service charge of 10–15 percent; sometimes your bill will state '*service non compris*' (service not included) in which case you will need to add the appropriate amount. At petrol stations it is customary to tip an attendant 2–3F or sometimes more, depending on the service performed. A hotel porter will normally receive 3–5F per bag, a maid 15–20F per week and a taxi driver 10–15 percent of the fare. But use discretion and tip according to the service you receive.

Museums and Galleries

Opening hours of museums and galleries do vary, so check before you go. The norm is 10.00–12.00 and 14.00–18.00, although out of season opening hours are often shorter. They invariably close on Mondays. Admission prices range from two to ten francs with guided tours starting from around 10F. On Sundays admission is often free.

The region is full of historical and artistic monuments and museums; churches and galleries abound and are not restricted to the major centres. Art lovers are particularly well catered for; from the medieval collection in the Palace of the Popes at Avignon to the many legacies of the Impressionists and their successors dotted around the Mediterranean coast the range is extensive. You can see Paul Cezanne's studio at Aix-en-Provence, Picasso paintings at Antibes and drawings at Arles, Matisse paintings in Nice and a fine collection of modern art at Cagnes-sur-mer.

Public Holidays

French national holidays occur with greater frequency than in the U.K. or U.S.A. and are meticulously observed. They fall as follows: — New Year's Day (January 1), Easter Monday (moveable), Labour Day (May 1), V E Day (May 8), Ascension Day (moveable), Whit Monday (moveable), Bastille Day (July 14), Assumption Day (August 15), All Saints Day (November 1), Remembrance Day (November 11) and Christmas Day (December 25).

Shopping

Shops, both large and small, offer an abundance of produce and merchandise from the chic boutiques on the St Tropez waterfront to the village grocery store — and you can be sure of attentive and personal service. Supermarkets and the extension of this idea, the Hypermarkets which incorporate shops of all descriptions and are springing up throughout the region, offer an extensive range of food and consumer goods of a surprisingly high quality. Provision shops are normally open from 07.00–18.30/19.30, others open a little later at 08.30 or 09.00. In smaller towns and villages you will often find that shops close between 12.00 and 14.00 — siesta time, which is still a strongly observed custom in the South of France. A good number of shops close all day Monday.

If you are self-catering, experiment with the local produce — the quality and variety of cheeses, wines, fruit and *charcuterie* (processed meats) are excellent. Other good local buys include perfumes and soaps (Grasse is the centre of the French perfume industry), liqueurs, pottery, silk scarves and many articles carved in olive wood. For the more indulgent (and affluent) French tailoring and jewellery is displayed with tempting effect in the fine shops of Cannes, Nice and Monte Carlo. Local arts and crafts are well represented in the hundreds of small galleries throughout the South.

Post Offices are open weekdays from 08.00 – 19.00 and from 08.00 – 12.00 on Saturdays. To telephone the U.K., dial 19, wait for the continuous dialling tone and then dial 44 followed by your S.T.D. code but omitting the first 0 of the number.

Sporting Facilities

The sea itself provides enormous scope for sporting activities, from a leisurely swim to scuba diving, snorkelling, wind-surfing, sailing and water-skiing. There are good facilities for these sports, but particularly on the Côte d'Azur. Good beaches abound with the exception of the area from the mouth of the Rhône to Marseilles. The open, sandy beaches of Roussillon are ideal for families with children, the only drawback being the narrow approach roads which tend to jam up in the high season. The coast between Marseilles and

Toulon – Côte des Calanques – an attractive stretch of steep limestone cliffs with many safe and sandy inlets, offers good resort and beach facilities, particularly at Bandol and Sanary. Further east along the Côte des Maures and the Esterel (with its pitted, red porphyry rocks), there are delightful beaches at Le Lavandou, St-Tropez and St-Raphaël. With a few exceptions – Antibes is one – the beaches on the Riviera coast, particularly in the large resorts, leave something to be desired.

Unfortunately, pollution remains a problem, particularly on the Riviera coast, but at least it is recognised today and the authorities are working hard to repair the damage done over the past decades through industrial waste and un-treated sewage. Nonetheless, the Côte d'Azur is still one of the most polluted areas in the Mediterranean and you should take care to check the water if you swim away from recognised beaches.

Although there is little chance of good sea fishing, inland there are lakes, rivers and mountain streams to provide excellent sport for the angler (you will normally require a permit). Golf and tennis are popular and very well catered for, particularly around Cannes, Nice and Monte Carlo. For winter sports enthusiasts there is good skiing in both the Alpes Maritime (Valberg, Beuil, and Pra-Loup) and the Pyrénées (Mont-Louis and Ax-les-Thermes). If you feel like entering into the spirit of things, try the local game of *boules*, a version of bowls. If possible, take any sports equipment with you as it tends to be expensive in France.

Tourist Offices and Consulates

Make as much use as possible of the many local tourist offices – *syndicats d'initiative* – which provide a very helpful service for the visitor, including free brochures, maps and hotel information. Principal offices on the coast are: – Nice: Gare Centrale, Avenue Thiers and in Marseilles: 4, Canebière.

Consulates are located as follows: –
United Kingdom: 24, avenue du Prado, Marseilles 6, tel. 53 43 32
U.S.A.: 9, rue Armeny, Marseilles 6, tel. 33 78 33 and at 3, rue du Dr. Baréty, Nice, tel. 88 89 55.

And before you travel don't forget to pick up as much information as you can from the French Government Tourist Offices located in most capital cities.

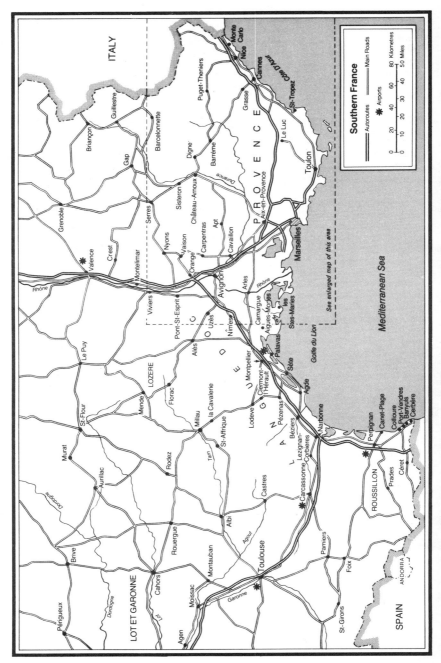

Southern France

Autoroutes — Main Roads

Airports ✳

| Kilometres | 0 | 20 | 40 | 60 | 80 |
| Miles | 0 | 10 | 20 | 30 | 40 | 50 |

ITALY

Monte Carlo
Nice
Cannes
Puget-Théniers
Grasse
Le Luc
St-Tropez
Toulon

Briançon
Guillestre
Gap
Barcelonnette
Digne
Barrême
Château-Arnoux
Sisteron
P R O V E N C E
Aix-en-Provence

Grenoble
Serres
Nyons
Vaison
Apt
Carpentras
Cavaillon
Crest
Valence ✳
Montélimar
Orange
Avignon
Arles
Marseilles

Rhône
Durance
Rhône

Viviers
Pont-St-Esprit
Uzès
Nîmes
Camargue
Aigues-Mortes
les
Stes-Maries
Palavas
Sète

Le Puy
Alès
LOZÈRE
Florac
Montpellier
Clermont-l'Hérault
Agde

Mende
la Cavalerie
Lodève
Pézenas
Béziers
Narbonne

St-Flour
Millau
St-Affrique
Lézignan-Corbières

Murat
Rodez
Castres
Carcassonne ✳
Aurillac
Rouergue
Albi
Tarn
Agout

Brive
Montauban
Toulouse ✳
Pamiers
Foix

Périgueux
Cahors
Moissac
Garonne
St-Girons

Dordogne
Dordogne
Lot
Agen
LOT ET GARONNE

SPAIN
ANDORRA

Prades
Céret
ROUSSILLON
Perpignan
Canet-Plage
Collioure
Port-Vendres
Banyuls
Cerbère

Mediterranean Sea

Golfe du Lion

Côte d'Azur

See enlarged map of this area

Cahors Bridge, Lot

Lot and the Roussillon

Cahors

There seem to me several good reasons for regarding Cahors as one of the main gateways to the South of France. Once you leave Perigord and the Dordogne behind, and the valley of the Lot, with its links with Quercy and Rouergue, begins to conjure up such names as Montauban, Toulouse, Carcassonne and Perpignan, there is no longer any doubt about it – the south is in the air. Moreover, Cahors itself already has something of the quality of a southern town and, in its own way, is as well known as Avignon for its bridge, but the Pont Valentré at Cahors is still intact.

Another aspect of Cahors with a half-way southern quality is the Boulevard Leon Gambetta, main street of the heart of the town, which roughly divides the very old from the comparatively recent. It is a pleasant, tree-lined street, with enough curve in its climb to add interest, and wide pavements with one-storey shops backed by well-proportioned houses, flats, or business and administrative premises.

Cahors is, too, a finger pointing southwards. The city is folded in a meander of the Lot in the way the Isle of Dogs is wrapped round by the Thames, and my only regret is that the Pont Valentré is on the western side of the city, instead of providing the north-south crossing of the Lot, where it would have made a more perfect gateway to the south.

Founded on the site of a spring which still provides drinking water, the settlement which became Cahors flourished under the Gauls and the Romans, acquiring the inevitable status symbols of forum, theatre, temples and baths within the indispenable protection of ramparts. But its period of greatest prosperity came in the 13th century under the Lombards, who eventually made Cahors one of the most important banking (i.e. money-lending) centres of Europe.

The Pont Valentré is far from being the only one of the city's ancient glories to delight the traveller. The 12th century Cathedral of St Etienne, with its two cupolas; the remaining towers and battlements of the city's ramparts; the 15th century Collège Pellegri; the splendid 16th century Maison de Roaldès (also known as the house of Henri IV); and the network of medieval and Renaissance houses in the old town are all well worth a leisurely tour. Don't miss the narrow streets by the Hôtel de Ville, on the east side of the Boulevard Leon Gambetta – the Rue Fondue Basse, the Rue de l'Université, and so on. The radiance of the true south, which penetrates even the narrowest and shadiest streets of the towns and villages of Provence, gives way here in the Lot to a real sense of the hard facts of medieval life, and you realise that, although in Cahors you are entering the south, you have not yet left the sombre north entirely behind.

The Syndicat d'Initiative, Place Aristide Briand, offers an admirable programme of excursions from June to September, spread out over the week, and contingent only on at least four persons applying for tickets in advance. Special excursions can be arranged and mopeds and bicycles are available for daily hire. For the motorist, route information and guidance is abundantly available. Characteristic among the day-trips (leaving Cahors at 08.30 and returning about 20.30) is the "Four Marvels" run, which takes in St Cirq-Lapopie, described as the most beautiful village in France; Cabrerets and the grotto of Pech-Merle; the world-famous caves of Padirac, and Rocamadour.

Cahors has a good range of reasonably priced hotels, with the Hôtel de France, Ambassadeurs, Mon Auberge and Melchior (all two-star) in the lead and at least a dozen modest but entirely adequate smaller hotels. It is worth remembering that in France hotels with somewhat unprepossessing exteriors in modest side-streets are often spotless, efficient, well run and, at today's prices, comparatively cheap. The Taverne restaurant, close by the Hôtel de Ville, is popular.

If you enjoy spending hours underground, being conducted through caves adorned with some of the richest graphic treasures of pre-history, the opportunities here are among the most rewarding in France: if you prefer to stay aboveground and enjoy the countryside and villages of today there are innumerable gentler and less exhausting trips to be made. A delightful example is to travel from Cahors along the valley of the Lot by bus, for instance; at Cabrerets you can relax in the delightful Hôtel des Grottes and the surrounding countryside, or simply walk up through the woods to

Pech-Merle (but check on the opening hours first). In fact the bus from Cahors, which replaces the single-track rail-car (autorail) of a few years ago, takes you only as far as Conduché, where you can then get a taxi to Cabrerets, or better still, walk the beautiful four kilometres by the side of the river Célé.

In every direction from Cahors are stretches of attractive countryside, quiet old villages and small towns, historic houses, great and small, and prehistoric sites. It gives the impression of an almost biblical mixture of fertile land and rich resources in food and wine, rocky plateaux (*les causses*) and awe-inspiring volcanic cliffs. For the claustrophobic traveller it is worth remembering that the Lot does not normally run to gorges: more often there is a dramatic cliff one side of the river and open, sunlit fields and vineyards on the other. The valley does, however, attract occasional heavy rainstorms, and the riverside villages are as quiet at night as the beginning of the world except where they are close to the excellent minor roads where, at the peak of the holiday season, the alternation of dazzling headlamps and total blackness does not encourage night or evening walks. Locally, spring and autumn are recommended as the ideal seasons for weather and general atmosphere. The famous Cahors wine is enjoyable at all seasons, particularly the *vieux* Cahors. It is said that Cahors wine was supplied to Tsarist Russia for use as communion wine, and in the Soviet Union today communion wine is still described as "vin de Cahors" – wherever it comes from.

Tarn and Garonne

Southwards from Cahors the N20 goes through the Tarn-et-Garonne Department towards Montauban and Toulouse. A more relaxed way of going there, for railway buffs, is by the "Capitole" express from Paris to Toulouse.

To the east lie the enchanting small towns and chateaux of Rouergue, the Aveyron river and department and, even farther east, the Cevennes National Park, of which more later. Eastward, too, is Conques-en-Rouergue, with its 11th century church of Sainte Foy, houses ranging from the 9th to the 15th centuries, and 14th century bridge, and Rodez, a treasure-store of Gothic and Renaissance architecture. But instead of ticking off these places on a list, try to time your trip so that you arrive in the cathedral square or more modest central *place* without attempting to place each astonishing survival from the Middle Ages or earlier in its precise half-century, and enjoy the colours of the surrounding stonework, the incomparable feeling of half a millennium of human habitation, the plane-tree shade, the unhurried footsteps and the evening sense of ingathering from the countryside.

Moissac

A desirable diversion on your southbound route, before you push on from Montauban, is to follow the N127 westward from Montauban to Moissac, on the N113 from Bordeaux which joins the N20 at Grisolles, between Montauban and Toulouse.

Moissac is a must, particularly in September, for the combination of its architectural treasures and the incomparable Chasselas grapes – with which goes an excellent local *cuisine* – though one cannot go far wrong in June, July and August, either, so rich is the variety of fruit in the area. Above all Moissac is noted for the magnificent 7th century abbey, which has the largest, and in some ways the finest, cloister in France, and, at the threshold of the abbey church of St Pierre, one of the most splendid groupings of Romanesque sculpture, to say nothing of the extraordinary pre-Gothic brick vaulting in the upper room of the narthex.

Founded, according to tradition, by Clovis in the year 506, affiliated with Cluny in 1053, badly damaged during the war against the Albigenses, of which tragedy we shall hear more as we go deeper into Languedoc, handed over to the King of England during the Hundred Years War in 1361 (to be recaptured in 1369), from being a staging-post for the pilgrims to Compostella, Moissac's abbey has become one of the most rewarding stages on the tourist's route. Apart from all historical, archaeological or religious interest, the sheer beauty of the great doorway, and of the sculptured heads of the prophets Jeremiah, St Peter and St John, is breathtaking.

Montauban and Albi

And so back to the road south at Montauban (pop. 48,555), a busy market-town at an important cross-roads between south-central and deep southern France built in the pinkish brick of Lower Quercy. It was founded in 1144 on the right bank of the Tarn by the Comte de Toulouse as a stronghold for the people of the earlier settlement of Montauriol, who had suffered greatly at the hands of the Abbé of Montauriol and the local lordlings. Montauban withstood a three months' siege by Louis XIII's Catholic army in 1621. But this success was short-lived: in 1628 the city fell without firing a shot and its fortifications were demolished.

Montauban, birthplace of the early 19th century French painter Ingres – the Ingres Museum has an excellent collection of the work of Ingres, and of Bourdelle, another native-son – has many attractive features. The red-brick museum; the arcaded Place Nationale with its morning flower market; the fortified church of St Jacques, with its 13th century bell-tower; Notre Dame cathedral; and the Old Bridge built entirely of brick at the beginning of the 14th century – all these make up an ensemble of considerable charm by the Tarn. Moreover, Montauban is the centre of a thriving fruit-growing area, whose public-relations experts have the pleasant habit of offering samples of fruit in season to visiting tourists.

East of Montauban the most important local digression is to Albi; N99 and N88, about 113 km (70 miles), not only for the magnificence of the 13th century cathedral of Ste Cécile, and the medieval bridge and houses, but also for the Toulouse-Lautrec Museum in the Palais de la Berbie, Place de l'Archevêché, which houses the most important collection in the world of the painter's works. His birthplace, in the Hôtel du Bosc, is open mornings and afternoons in the summer: in spring and autumn only for parties, on request.

Albi, capital of the Tarn Department and ancient Gallo-Roman capital of the Albigenses, stands on the left bank of the Tarn river. The old city, dominated by the cathedral, forming one of the most picturesque architectural complexes in southern France, with a wealth of warm-coloured brick and fine timber-work. The decorated ceiling of the cathedral – itself a masterpiece of French Gothic in brick – is worth a special visit. The main structure was built between 1282 and 1400, the church was consecrated in 1480 and the splendid group of sculpture which forms, in the middle of the nave, the gallery and choir-screen, was completed about 1500. Between 1509 and 1514 Italian painters were called in to carry out the frescoes on walls and ceiling vaults. (Syndicat d'Initiative: 19 Place Ste Cécile.)

Toulouse

Back to the N20 to resume the journey south from Montauban, and so to Toulouse, France's fourth biggest city (pop. 400,000), capital of the Haute-Garonne Department and home of the French Concorde. Red roofs, pale red brick, masses of greenery, an abundance of fine architecture ranging from the 11th to the 18th centuries, and a central cluster of buildings round the great Romanesque church of St Sernin, all give the impression, in aerial photographs, of the heart of a country cathedral town rather than a great artistic and industrial centre. Every facility for holidaymakers of all kinds and ages. Call first at the S.I. in the Donjon du Capitole, where you will find one of the most comprehensive programmes of excursions of any city in the south.

Not only has Toulouse one of the most impressive lists of hotels in France outside Paris, including three four-star and one four-star plus, the city also offers a reassuring range of more modest accommodation and makes a point of helping visitors to find reasonable family lodgings or rooms where they can do their own cooking, to say nothing of the wide range of camping and caravan sites. There are, too, opportunities of finding places to stay in many attractive smaller centres within a range of 28 to 64 km of Toulouse, such as Lavour, Gaillac, Montauban, and Albi. Horse-drawn caravans can be hired on a weekly basis for a leisurely tour of the region.

Toulouse has six theatres, of which the best known are the Capitole, the Daniel Sorano and the Grenier, and two first-rank orchestras. It is linked to London by a direct Air France service to Heathrow.

Carcassonne

From Toulouse the N113 leads to Carcassonne, 91 km (57 miles). I count myself fortunate in having seen Carcassonne for the first time many years ago from a train in the early hours of the morning. All I can recall in the remembered half-light is the outline of the old city in the distance, but it was unforgettable, and nothing that has happened since then can erase, or alter, that memory. Even today neither crowds nor trinket shops can destroy the beauty and the power of this unique survival.

The Lower Town, incorporating the ancient commercial and bourgeois districts, with its main boulevards on the lines of the old ramparts, is on the left bank, reached by the Pont Neuf and the Pont Vieux. The Old City, on a bluff on the right bank of the Aude, has preserved the most remarkable medieval fortified enclosure in Europe. Its structure – one of the world's greatest gifts to historians and archaeologists – ranges from huge Gallo-Roman stone blocks securely interlocked, without mortar, to the Royal walls of rectangular grey stones of the age of St Louis. Within this range there are the cubic stones of the Visigoths, alternating with brick courses, and, from ducal times, sandstone blocks assembled in roughly shaped masses. And if the centuries appear to have become mixed, much of this was due to the excavation, and removal to other parts, of the structure of lower depths of walling during the creation of the upper and lower tiltyards.

The Old City stands on an escarpment which attracted the Romans from the 1st century BC because of its commanding position between the Mediterranean and Toulouse. The Visigoths seized it for the same reason in the 5th century AD and built a new defence wall, and three centuries later the Franks took over. For 400 years Carcassonne was a prosperous local capital, until, in the 13th century, its peace was broken by the Crusade against the Albigensians, which brought so much devastation and bloodshed to Languedoc, where the religious reform movement was strongest.

Two hundred thousand Frenchmen from the north, under the command of Simon de Montfort, prepared to drive the "heretics" from Languedoc, and, after sacking Béziers, laid siege to Carcassonne. The defence of the city was organised by Count Raymond VI of Toulouse and his 24-year-old son Raymond-Roger. Raymond-Roger, lured from the fortress to negotiate with a false promise of safe-conduct, was seized as soon as he reached de Montfort's camp, chained, and thrown into prison. The defenders of Carcassonne, near to famine, lost heart and de Montfort seized the city, where Raymond-Roger died six months later, prisoner in a dungeon of his own city.

Louis XI of France (St Louis) caused the houses which had been built at the foot of the ramparts to be razed to the ground and the rebellious inhabitants of the city paid for their faith with seven years' expulsion to the other side of the river, where they built what is now the Lower Town.

From then on the Old City became an impregnable fortress. During the Hundred Years War the Black Prince had to give up any idea of taking the city and be content with setting fire to the Lower Town. After 1659, with Roussillon annexed to France, not Carcassonne but Perpignan became the frontier defence against Spain, and the city might well have been allowed to decline, or even to be demolished. With the revival of interest in the Middle Ages in the 19th century, however, the French government entrusted the restoration of Carcassonne to Viollet-le-Duc, and the work continues today.

The best way into the city is by the Porte d'Aude, on foot, leaving your car near the church of St Gimer. The Porte d'Aude is on the west side of the city, facing the Lower Town. There is parking space, on the other hand, by the Porte Narbonnaise, on the east side, where entry to the city is by a drawbridge. For details of guided visits, lecture tours and the admission charges, apply to the Château Comtal. The upper and lower tiltyards can be visited without charge; a stroll there gives excellent views of the city.

The Lower Town has a good collection of paintings (including some Chardin still-lifes) in the Musée des Beaux Arts, Rue de Verdun, which also has interesting material relating to Andre Chénier, the revolutionary poet whose childhood was spent in Carcassonne and who died on the scaffold in 1794. The Syndicat d'Initiative, in the Boulevard Camille-Pelletan (Lower Town), is given three-star rating in the Government's official list.

Perpignan

Perpignan, 118 km (74 miles) from Carcassonne by the N118 and N117, is in some ways the most exotic town in the South of France. The charm of the other cities in the sun comes from a mixture of reminders of the antique world, the enclosed nature of medievalism, the French village *place* with its trees and soft-coloured walls and midday balm. Perpignan is different. It has most of the qualities of the other towns, but with an additional flavour, an extra dimension. Parts are reminiscent of other French towns, but the main impression – or so I find – conveys more of Spain and North Africa than of Rome or the Franks, a Spanish–Arab mixture of intense heat, intense colour and intensely black shadow.

Time was when one discovered Perpignan on the way to Collioure or Banyuls, or because one had caught a glimpse of the magic of Roussillon. Recently it has become the last chance for motorists to fill up with French milk and honey before heading for the oil and paella of the popular new resorts of Spain. It can be overcrowded with transit traffic and unbearably hot in the eye of August, but its ageless qualities make it uniquely fascinating.

It is almost 30 years since I first wandered by chance through a short tunnel in the earthworks near the local barracks and the ancient citadel and found myself in the incredible courtyards of the Palace of the Kings of Majorca. The restoration of this splendid survival had, in fact, only just begun three years previously, and the impact was, perhaps, even greater then than it is on unprepared visitors today.

Historically, the site is of considerable interest in the tangled story of the separation and demarcation of nations. Roussillon, which in the 2nd century BC was part of the great Roman province of the Narbonnaise, became, after invasions by Visigoths and Arabs, a bone of contention between France and Spain. Pepin the Short wrested it from the Arabs in the 8th century and subjected it to the Count of Barcelona. It was handed over, by the last hereditary Count of Barcelona, to the King of Aragon in 1172. In the 13th century, Jacques I of Aragon, who had captured the Balearic Islands from the Moslems, made a gift of them to his son, along with Roussillon, Cerdagne and Montpellier. The son took the title of King of Majorca and made Perpignan his capital. In 1344, after three Kings of Majorca had reigned, Pierre IV of Aragon took over what was left of their territories.

But in spite of the extraordinary history of the palace, here again, as in so many parts of southern France, a visit is recommended for the interest and beauty of the building itself rather than for its historical importance. For most holidaymakers an attempt to associate the places they visit with remote and unfamiliar historical episodes is more exhausting than enjoyable. Only if one comes across a site that suddenly brings to life a fragment of history or literature which one has always found absorbing does the story behind it become as exciting as the spectacle itself. Most times it is better to respond simply to the thing in itself – the building, the panorama and so on – to its visual charm or interest, or merely to the fact that you came across it on a fine day when all was going well.

The Palace of the Kings of Majorca is very much a thing in itself, a splendid example of royal architecture of the 13th and 14th centuries, with a magnificent square courtyard flanked by a double gallery with a series of arcades. Entry to the courtyard is through great arches, which themselves support an elegant loggia of six Gothic arcades from the second half of the 14th century. At the far end of the courtyard the 'Paradise' gallery is supported by the wide arches of the lower gallery, and other arcades, Romanesque and Gothic, add to the elegance of the whole structure: the Gothic elements, particularly in the arcaded bell-tower, are comparatively rare in the Roussillon of that period.

But the Palace of the Kings of Majorca is not all Perpignan has to offer. The three-star S.I. is at 3, cité Bartissol, where excellent maps and guides to the city's many other attractions are available.

Le Castillet (south side of the Place de la Victoire), a fortress in dark-red brick that gives a Spanish–African flavour to the heart of the city and contains in the Casa Pairal a museum of Catalan arts and folk-lore (open every day except Saturday afternoon and Sunday in winter); La Loge de Mer (14th to 16th centuries), created originally as a finance market or exchange (*bourse*) and a Sea Consulate or *tribunal de commerce maritime*: this is one of a complex of buildings ranging from the 13th to the 15th centuries which includes the old Palais de Justice and the Hôtel de Ville. The Place de la Loge has been opened out and some improvements made in a manner that befits the heart of the city, with its cafés and charming custom among the young people of dancing the *sardane* in the square on summer evenings. Also worth seeing are the Cathédrale St Jean (1324), the Musée Rigaud in the buildings of the ancient university, the Jardins St Jacques, and the Pépinière.

There is a wide range of hotels, pensions and restaurants, and within easy reach are St-Vicens and the Château de Salses. The former Canet-Plage (Perpignan is only 13 km from the sea by the N617) is now the grandly re-titled holiday complex Canet-en-Roussillon St Nazaire, with a vast beach 9 km long and 100 metres wide shelving gently into the sea. A pleasure port with over 750 berths, there is every conceivable facility for sport and exercise, games, hotels, gambling, flats, villas and studios and, if all this is not enough (or too much), a quiet, beautiful hinterland.

Of the three dozen or so hotels of all categories the top-grade Grand Hotel (Quai Sadi-Carnot), the Hôtel le Catalogne (24 Cours Lazare-Escarguel), its rather less expensive neighbour the Delseny (14 Cours Lazare-Escarguel), and the Hôtel de la Loge are well recommended. There is also a wide choice in the two-star and one-star brackets. They all offer discount rates for off-season bookings.

But for those who hanker after old places and old ways for holidays one of the great assets of Perpignan is its comparative proximity to Collioure, Port Vendres, Banyuls and Cerbère.

Collioure

Collioure, in spite of rapid expansion (it is still officially credited with only 2600 permanent inhabitants), remains one of the most picturesque fishing ports of the whole Mediterranean coast of France from Cerbère to Menton. It consists, in fact, of two small ports, separated by the huge mass of the ancient

Templars' Castle, which is balanced pictorially (seen from the sea) by the tough-looking 16th century church with its feet in the water which is built on to an old lighthouse converted into a clock-tower with a charming pink cupola. Behind the church, which is in the Old Part, lie the narrow streets and alleys of the old town (the Quartier du Mouré). The seaward wall of the town has two gateways giving access to and from the port.

Collioure shares with Cerêt an honoured place in the history of modern painting and was much favoured by Matisse, Derain, Dufy, Juan Gris and many others. It has half a dozen hotels (the Hôtellerie des Templiers has an interesting permanent collection of paintings) and, in addition, a number of restaurants.

Fishing "au lamparo" – that is with a lamp in the bows of the boat – is still carried on. Do not miss a trip to the Hermitage of Notre-Dame de Consolation (about five km) for the beauty of the site and the unforgettable crystal purity of the natural spring there – the most wonderful water I have ever tasted. I must admit that I came to it just before noon on a scorching hot day after spending a long morning learning something about the care of vines from a friendly fisherman of Collioure who had a tiny vineyard in the hills above the town: on the way back, with basket-loads of grapes, we found refreshment at the hermitage and its unforgettable spring. The way to the hermitage is to take the N114 in the direction of Argelès. About one km from Collioure, at the top of the first slope, turn left into the D86 and follow this for just over three km until, at a cross-roads, you take the sharpest left. The site alone, with its views over Collioure, is worth the trip. (About five km in all.)

Port Vendres

About three km from Collioure towards the Spanish frontier is Port Vendres, a pleasant small port for passenger and car-ferry services to Algeria and Morocco, combined with a fishing port, facilities for pleasure boats, and a beach nearby. Between them Collioure and Port Vendres muster about two dozen hotels, some open all the year round, and several restaurants. The passenger port is a rectangular basin in which a delightful way of spending time can be to sit on the terrace of a waterfront café and watch some of the bigger ships berth with inches (literally) to spare. Although the name means "Port of Venus" the cult of Venus does not seem to be any more insistent there than anywhere else along the coast.

Banyuls-sur-Mer

Banyuls-sur-Mer, about seven km nearer Spain, prides itself on being the most southerly holiday resort of France's Mediterranean coast. It is also the birth-place of the great sculptor Aristide Maillol and the home of Banyuls, a full-bodied wine (sometimes compared with port) grown on the nearby slopes which are terraced with dry-stone walls. All in all it is, and has long been, an excellent family holiday centre, at the heart of the Côte Vermeille, with every type of sport and recreation within reach, 12 km of bays and creeks, a pleasant Catalan hinterland, and an excellent choice of hotels, flats, studios and camping sites. The helpful S.I. is at the Mairie, and the research station for marine biology has an excellent aquarium open to the public, where you can come face to face with that curious fish, the *rascasse*.

Cerbère

The French Mediterranean coast ends 10 km farther on at Cerbère, the frontier town between the French Côte Vermeille of Roussillon and the Costa Brava of Spain. Cerbère has a good sandy beach, some good hotels and pensions (S.I. at the Mairie), and good opportunities for camping. Basically a small fishing port in an inlet sheltered to the north by Cap Canadell and to the south by Cap Cerbère, it is a pleasant spot and an important international rail point.

Perpignan is also the ideal base for excursions into the Pyrénées Orientales; to the delightful health resort of Amélie-les-Bains, under the shadow of Mount Canigou (2785 metres); Prades with its music festival associated with the late Pablo Casals, the great Spanish cellist; Cérêt; the magnificent monastery of St Michel de Cuxa; the castle of Montségur; and, farther west, Foix, in the Ariège, one of the most picturesque of all the medieval towns of France.

Hotel d'Alfonce,
Pézenas

Lozère and Languedoc

South through the Cevennes

Between Auvergne and the Mediterranean lies some of the most beautiful, varied and, in places, mysterious countryside in the South of France. Here are the gorges of the Tarn and the Cevennes, the strange *Causses* and mirage villages which turn out to be rock formations, stretches of harsh but fragrant moorland, sun-baked and bleached in some places, green and luxuriant in others, sweeping down through olive and mulberry groves to vast vineyards, salt-marshes, lagoons, and the sea. The heart of the area may be roughly defined by a line taken from Mende (Lozère), through Millau (Aveyron), Lodève and Béziers, Sete and Montpellier (Hérault), Nîmes and Ales (Gard), back to Mende.

The *Causses*, which begin south of the Monts d'Aubrac and Mende, and contain the Gorges du Tarn, lie between the valley of the Lot (to the north), the Cevennes (to the east), Rouergue (to the west), and the Hérault and the lower Languedoc (to the south). Product of something like 500 million years of strains and stresses in the earth's crust, they now present a strange landscape of dry, rocky plateaux through which the Tarn, the Jonte and the Dourbie flow at the bottom of deep canyons.

The climate on the plateaux, which average about 1000 metres above sea-level, is hot and dry in summer, harsh with a long snow season and strong winds in winter – with little to temper the force of the wind. There have always been small villages and settlements in sheltered corners, and sheep make the most of the sparse vegetation, providing wool for the textile industry of the towns, fertiliser for the soil, and milk for the world-famous Roquefort cheese. And it is in this region that one comes across extraordinary rock formations which, from a distance, look so much like ancient villages that they have been given such names as Montpellier-le-Vieux and Nîmes-le-Vieux . . . But do not imagine that you will come across these in your travels in the way they must have once suddenly appeared before the gaze of earlier visitors; Montpellier-le-Vieux, for example (its full title is "Le Chaos de Montpellier-le-Vieux"), which is 18 km (11 miles) north-east of Millau, can be visited only from the Maubert café-restaurant, which is off the D111 from Millau. There you pay about 1 fr. 50 for an entry ticket which allows you to drive about a mile along a private road to a vast parking lot, from which you can explore the site on foot.

These "natural ruins" are said to have been brought about by the association in the same rock masses of soluble calcium carbonate and insoluble magnesium carbonate. Chemical erosion by water finding its way deviously among the soluble areas of the rocks has carved out extraordinary ruined towers, arcades, bluffs and alleyways, while the clay residue from the soluble rocks has given a foot-hold to the vegetation which adds charm and verisimilitude to these "ruined villages", enhanced in some areas by the proximity of actual dwellings. At the Cirque de Mourèze, for example, eight km west of Clermont l'Hérault, the ancient village of Mourèze stands amid enormous blocks of dolomite rock eroded into fantastic shapes.

Other fine examples of this geological phenomenon in the region are at Arcs-de-St-Pierre, Ruquesaltes and Rajol.

The canyons through which the Tarn, the Jonte and the Dourbie flow draw visitors from all over the world, offering some of the most awe-inspiring and dramatic landscapes in Europe. Moreover, with great cliffs sheltered from the winds, often turned to catch the maximum amount of sunlight, and great layers of marl exposed, the cliff-sides and the alluvial banks of the rivers lend themselves to extensive cultivation with all the beauty and softening of aspect this brings.

As the waters find their way down through the *Causses* to the impermeable layers they create a whole underground network of pools and streams which eventually emerge in springs and waterfalls. This has led to the creation of many beautiful grottoes and caves which are accessible to tourists. Among these are the Aven Armand, the Grotte des Demoiselles, and the Grotte de Clamouse (near St-Guilhem-le-Desert, of which more later). Dargilan and Bramabiau are among the best known.

You could still do much worse than prepare yourself for the Cevennes with Robert Louis Stevenson's *Travels with a Donkey*. Neither tourism nor road 'improvements' have yet fundamentally altered the character of the country-side, and there is no cause for regret in the fact that the legendary "Beast of Gevaudon" is no longer roaming the hills and forests.

Since the end of the 19th century systematic re-afforestation has compensated largely for the denuding of the woodland by the charcoal-burning glassmakers who caused havoc among the beeches, and by the great flocks of sheep which, in their seasonal migrations from the lower Languedoc to the Cevennes and the *Causses*, cropped the young leaves and shoots over a wide track.

The highest peaks, Mount Lozère (1702 metres) and Mount Aigoual (1567 metres), offer fine views when the weather is right, and you do not have to travel far down to reach an agreeable and smiling countryside of oaks, heather, chestnut forests and villages. Then come well-watered orchards and alpine greenery. The lower valleys bring us down from the Cevennes to the Mediterranean, through a truly southern region of strong sun, vineyards, olives, mulberry and lavender.

Mende

Mende is a good place from which to explore southwards through the Cevennes, the gorges of the Tarn and the Jonte, by way of the massif of the Aigoual to the valley of the Hérault. Mende, prefecture of Lozère, with a population of well over 10,000 and 12 hotels, ranging from modest to first class, is not only a good centre from which to find one's way about Lozère and the *Causses*, but also an agreeable small town in itself, situated as it is in the upper valley of the Lot, with its cathedral (restored in the 17th century), its ancient bridge (Pont Notre-Dame), museum of archaeology and folk-lore, magnificent views from the Belvedere of the nearby Mount Mimat. (S.I. 16, Blvd du Soubeyran.)

For the heart of the Cevennes take the N107 from Mende to Florac, a pleasant little town on the Tarnon river, at the foot of dolomite cliffs, amid gardens and orchards, with four or five hotels and some furnished apartments if you are tempted to stay a few days and explore locally. Then continue along the N107 to St-Laurent-de-Treves, where you pick up the N583 to Le Rey. From Le Rey you follow the magnificent Corniche des Cevennes (D9) for about 40 km (25 miles) to St-Jean-du-Gard: one of those drives which, given the afternoon light and not too much other traffic, make you feel that this trip alone would have made your visit to France worth while.

For the gorges of the Tarn, which run between the Causse de Sauveterre and the Causse Méjean, check in at the S.I. in Mende for your best route, according to season, time of day and whether you prefer grandiose or gentler scenery. The best route is probably by way of Balsièges and Molines to Ste-Enimie and Le Rozier, taking in a visit to the Point Sublime, but there is so much of beauty and interest to see that you could explore fruitfully for weeks.

Similarly, your routes farther south make a choice difficult, unless you have the time to explore all of them. One leads from Le Rozier by way of Montpellier-le-Vieux and Millau to the Cirque de Navacelles, then on to Lodève, Gignac and Montpellier (taking in the Cirque de Mourèze, near Clermont l'Hérault). Another is from St-Jean-du-Gard (where you left the Corniche des Cevennes) over the Col de l'Asclier (superb views, but only for the first-rate, careful driver), to the Grotte des Demoiselles and down the valley of the Hérault to St-Guilhem-le-Désert and the Grotte de Clamouse, and so to Montpellier.

St-Guilhem-le-Désert

The tiny village of St-Guilhem-le-Désert, in the Hérault Department, just over 32 km (20 miles) from Montpellier, with its abbey church dating from the 11th century, square tower, Roman houses and the remains of its surrounding ramparts, is one of the jewels of southern France. At the confluence of the Verdus and the Hérault, it is in a region of splendid gorges and has a backcloth of scarps dominated by the Château de Don Juan, or Château du Géant, as it is sometimes called. The abbey, round which the village is clustered, was founded in 804 by Guilhem, Duke of Acquitaine – the Guilhem d'Orange of the *Chansons de Geste* – but all that remains is the church, which was consecrated in 1076.

The splendid doorway, which faces the square shaded by a massive 100-year-old plane tree, is crowned by a 15th century bell-tower. The great apse, with its lovely colonnade under the tiled roof and its elegant supporting apses on either side, is a blend of strength and elegance, and both the abbey church and the surrounding houses are warm and radiant in gold-coloured stone with red and ochre roofs.

St-Guilhem has one small hotel, the Fonzès, which would make an excellent base for exploring the area, but you are not likely to find a room vacant if you arrive without warning between May and September.

For the grotto-seeker, Clamouse is just over a mile away to the south along the D4. The grottoes of the Sergeant and Baume Cellier are just over two miles away – *plus* a total of about 6 hours' walking (there and back) when you leave the D4. The path is on the left just over a mile after leaving St-Guilhem in the direction of Ganges and Montpellier.

Montpellier

Montpellier, in some ways one of the most pleasing cities of the south, is also one of the most interesting in its combination of historic interest and contemporary dynamism. The medieval heart of the old city, deeply scarred by the French Wars of Religion, became, under Louis XIV, the administrative capital of Languedoc and was enriched with some of the most elegant town houses in France in a veritable sunburst of contained urban development. In our own time, while the old city has been preserved for both day-to-day use and aesthetic enjoyment, the commercial, industrial, residential and educational sectors have been developed to meet a population growth of over 36 percent in the past decade.

What this means to the quality of the city as a place to visit includes the sense of youth and vitality given by not only one great university (with memories of Rabelais), but three; a new administrative centre only a few hundred yards from the old city in which the elegance of the new Mairie makes it a classic of modern architecture, and a series of residential and research centres encircling the old town, each of which contributes its own sense of architectural and social stimulus.

For holidays and leisure travel generally Montpellier has much to offer – not least an average of 300 sunny days a year and a mild winter. It is essentially a southern town with all the facilities for spending much of one's life in the open

Abbey of St Michel de Cuxa, Pyrenees

St Martin du Canigou, Pyrenees

air that that description implies. From the huge main square – the Place de la Comédie – a maze of busy narrow old streets climbs to the highest point of the city, which is crowned by an elegant, rectangular tree-lined terrace – the Peyrou. There is a local legend that the name comes from the old word for a heap of stones, and was first used to describe the site by the townspeople while the monumental terrace was being cleared and built during the 18th century. At the eastern end of the terrace is a magnificent triumphal arch in honour of Louis XIV, in the middle an equestrian statue of the same monarch, and at the western end an impressive 18th century water-tower. This water-tower marks the Montpellier end of a remarkable aqueduct, 880 metres (almost five-eighths of a mile) long and 22 metres (over 70 ft) high, which strides over the western outskirts of the city to bring water from a source at St-Clément and elsewhere. Built in the 18th century in two superimposed arcades, and inspired by the Pont du Gard, it is a dramatic sight to come across, whether first seen from the Peyrou or from the streets below.

The best time to climb the hill to the Peyrou (with its east–west axis), and to stroll along its walks – sometimes to the accompaniment of music from concealed sources in the gardens – is the evening, when the triumphal arch, which marks the highest point of the old city, is ablaze with the sunset.

On the more practical level Montpellier has a most efficient Syndicat d'Initiative (in the Place de la Comédie): a wide-ranging and more than adequate selection of moderately priced hotels and restaurants (the three universities, Montpellier I, II and III, are attended by something like 30,000 students); theatres, cinemas, concerts, wine festivals and museums, including the Fabre museum, which has an impressive collection of 19th and early 20th century French paintings. Frédéric Bazille, the French Impressionist painter who at one time looked after the young, impoverished Renoir, and whose tall figure is seen among the painters in "The Studio at the Batignolles" painted by Fantin-Latour in 1870 and now in the Louvre, is well represented in this museum. But check first whether his canvases are there or on loan to some other gallery in France. Even if they are missing, there is a marvellous cool Matisse, and some fine Corots and Courbets to console you.

Two points to watch in Montpellier. Be wary of the one-way traffic system in the outer boulevards, which, if you are not on the alert, may have you circling the centre of the town many times before you spot your turn into the old city. Do not be misled by the brave blue appearance on maps of the Verdanson, a tributary of the Lez, and the northern boundary of the old city: it is an empty, high-walled river-bed – empty, that is, except for the rubbish dumped in it.

Nîmes

If you drive to Nîmes from Montpellier by way of Vendargues, Lunel and Milhaud there is nothing, particularly in the last few miles, to prepare you for the magnificence that is Nîmes itself. True, you drive through apparently endless vineyards (competing with each other in their invitations to stop and taste the local product), but the last stretch is a gauntlet of roadway signs, massive billboards, petrol stations, garages, industrial sites and shacks, culminating in a residential industrial belt of total anonymity but unmistakably recent date.

Moreover, if you arrive in the Montpellier bus, except for an impressive glimpse of the Avenue Feuchères there is not a great deal, up to the moment you step off the bus, to indicate that you are only an easy stroll from some of the most exciting vistas in Europe.

But within a few minutes, by walking past the Esplanade and the Palais de Justice, you are brought up short by the Arènes – the best preserved of all the 70 Roman amphitheatres still to be found in the world.

The first glimpse of the great amphitheatre makes a curious impression. For one thing there is enough open space round it for one to be able to see it in something like perspective, and further, the sandy waste immediately close to it seems both ancient and homely for the marshalling of vast numbers of spectators who gather for the *corridas* that are held throughout the summer: all this, with posters of forthcoming *férias* which include both bullfights and *"courses à la cocarde"* (competitions to seize a rosette from the bull's horns and get away with it safely), creates an intimate, lived-in atmosphere round this incredible monument which, to me at least, conjures up the approaches of a football stadium rather than the survival of an ancient blood-sport. Indeed, for those of us who would like to see it put to a better human use than bull-baiting it is ironical to recall that at one period in its long history the amphitheatre was seized by poor squatters, who borrowed materials from the great mass of Roman masonry to build themselves homes and a chapel. The village in the arena at one time had 2000 inhabitants, and it was not until the 19th century that the debris of this occupation was finally cleared away.

Nîmes is a particularly good base for touring the countryside because of the number and variety of the hotels, ranging from the four-star Mapotel and Sofitel and the excellent Hôtel du Cheval Blanc and Novotel, through a good selection of medium-price hotels to many other modest but comfortable establishments. The Hôtel de la Maison Carrée is delightfully situated if you like, as I do, to stay in the very heart of a city you are visiting for the first time.

In the same way the Maison Carrée, that pleasantly domesticated mini-Parthenon, now crowded-in a little, in the friendliest possible way, by some of the city's most charming streets, has an appeal that owes less to Roman pomp, efficiency and brutality than to a Greek inspiration softened and humanised in the sun of southern France. It is always more enjoyable to be delighted rather than over-awed by ancient monuments, particularly on holiday: there is a limit to the extent and the frequency with which one can be dutifully impressed without longing for something light and more easily digested, and the elegance, grace, human scale and beautiful proportions of the Maison Carrée create immediately a feeling of pure enjoyment. This is enhanced by the small but admirable selection of items inside the building, which thus becomes a foretaste, or an extension, of the excellent Archaeological Museum in a former Jesuit college off the Blvd Admiral-Courbet.

Nîmes, which gave its name to the fabric denim, is a city in and around which one could easily spend a whole summer. The Fountain Gardens, created in the 18th century and crowned by La Tour Magne, probably France's most ancient monument, are cool and beautifully designed, the streets are magnificent and tree-lined, or intimate and charming, like those near the Maison Carrée, where, at 6, rue Auguste, you will find the S.I. In the same area of narrow streets you may, if you are fortunate, stumble on the pastrycook's shop of the *croquants de Villaret*, a shop that takes you back into an earlier world in the most magical way.

Nîmes is also within easy reach of the Pont du Gard, that most majestic Roman aqueduct, and of Uzès, seat of the Premier Duchy of France, and one of the most delightful of all the country towns of southern France, richly endowed with architectural treasures, a spring music festival and a pleasant countryside. The two-star S.I. at Uzès is in the Hôtel de Ville.

La Grande Motte

Montpellier is becoming more and more important as the natural base for visiting the new resorts of the Languedoc–Roussillon coast. The nearest, its pyramidal blocks of apartments visible from Montpellier–Fréjorgues airport, is La Grande Motte, where the architect Jean Balladur has created a series of temples to the sun which serve also – in principle – to screen the beaches from the prevailing winds. From the sea the dazzling white pyramids, or ziggurats, are said to suggest a part of the Cevennes. From the waterfront and the streets of La Grande Motte, and from Fréjorgues, they are undoubtedly impressive and they work well as sun-traps for every flat. Certainly no resorts could offer better holiday facilities for the yachtsman.

There are berths for well over 1000 boats in the three basins of the port, each berth with its water, power, telephone and television points. The town itself is kept clear of traffic except bright Californian-style small buses. As the original plan nears completion, the great blocks are being varied in size and shape, and hotel accommodation is integrated into the temples to the sun. Similar developments close to La Grande Motte are Carnon and Port Camargue; Port Camargue will eventually have berths for even more boats than La Grande Motte, and has great stretches of fine sand either side of the harbour. Some 55 km (34 miles) west of La Grande Motte is another important new holiday area, Cap d'Agde.

If you follow the coast road, N108, it takes you by way of the old port of Sète, and if the sight of the pleasant old town, backed by Mont St-Clair, tempts you to linger there rather than push on, I can hardly blame you. For Sète is a reminder of the kind of family holiday places many of us knew when we were very young – a fishing port which attracts tourists without allowing tourism to change the character of the town or its harbour. With two three-star hotels and about 30 others, and with trawlers, pleasurecraft, shops and a variety of excellent restaurants, as well as sandy beaches within reach, there is something for everybody. A good place from which to observe the busy life and movement among the restaurants of Sète's "Grand Canal" is an upstairs room in the pleasant Hotel de l'Orque Bleue, on the Quai de l'Aspirant Herber.

Cap d'Agde is well worth a visit, or a prolonged stay. I found it to be one of the most pleasing of all the new resorts. Old Agde, with its cathedral of volcanic rock, is fascinating; the Grau d'Agde, just west of Cap d'Agde, still has the paraphernalia of a fishing village, with boats, trawl-nets and wharves, and Cap d'Agde has been built with taste and vision like a typical Mediterranean fishing village; the colours and shapes and spaces on the waterfront and in the narrow streets, though carried out in concrete, are charming and relaxed. Farther along the coast towards Perpignan, Gruissan is attractively designed round an old centre, and is one of the most interestingly planned of the whole network of resorts. Lying among lagoons on what is almost an island site, and linked with the sea by a canal, the red-roofed old village clusters round the slopes of a rock on which stands the remains of Barbarossa's Tower. The village, with its own port and boatyard, and two or three pleasant restaurants, goes about its own quiet business only five minutes' walk from the new resort, with its apartment blocks, pleasure port, trawler berths, and the excellent two-star Hôtel le Corail in an ideal position for access to everything of interest.

After Gruissan comes the complex of La Franqui – Leucate Plage, Port Leucate and Port Barcarès. The Leucate–Barcarès complex is one of the most ambitious of the new holiday-resort developments of Languedoc–Roussillon. Port Leucate alone aims at the eventual provision of accommodation for about 40,000 beds in collective dwellings, camping and caravan sites, and holiday villages. The port, between the Mediterranean and the lagoon (l'Étang de Leucate), with miles of quays, berths, canals, basins, repair, lifting and maintenance services, covered berths and power, fuel and water points everywhere, already claims to be one of the best-equipped pleasure ports in Europe.

The achievement, through a mixture of public and private investment, is impressive. On what was once a kind of no-man's-land, between sea and inland waters, the mosquito-ridden flats formerly discouraged access to the lovely hinterland of the Corbières and the rest of the magnificent country from Narbonne to the Pyrénées and Spain. Now the mosquitoes have been disposed of, and in their place are houses, apartment clusters, whole villages, shopping centres, entertainment complexes, lots and lots of greenery and miles and miles and miles of sandy beaches.

Less dramatic than La Grande Motte, less successful than Cap d'Agde in re-creating the picturesque element of the old Mediterranean ports (largely because the natural configuration of Cap d'Agde justified the attempt to revive the colours and shapes of the older world), Port Leucate has its own qualities, to which the demand for flats, houses and other accommodation pays ample tribute. There is, perhaps inevitably, a confusion of styles. Attempts to recall Greek villages or the coloured cottages of the Roussillon clambering up the hillside are among the kind of architectural ideas that look better on the drawing board or in skilful photographs than they look on these largely unaccented flats of land, sand and water. But these are subjective reactions: the facts are that as holiday living-quarters these houses, villas, apartment blocks and villages offer a degree of comfort, convenience, efficiency and often interior style that is so far above the average of old-fashioned seaside accommodation that it is no surprise to discover that this is just what large communities of families with young children (mostly French and German, with some Dutch) have been seeking for years.

There are several hotels and restaurants in the port. Among the restaurants the Lamparo is particularly good – a splendid place to try the regional Listel wines.

Obviously, those who are still looking for the Collioure or Concarneau or Polperro of their childhood will not find it here. What they will find, if they come with open minds, are vast sandy beaches, hot sun with some wind to temper it, and a magnificent fusion of land and water with a hinterland of vineyards, hills and ancient castles and villages. There are facilities for physical recreation, child-minding, bathing in sun and sea and labour-free relaxation which offer a range of choice and a general level of built-in comfort and freedom for larger numbers of holidaymakers than have ever been provided before. How well the modish structures will weather over the years is another question, like the long-term problem of whether, in the long run, there will be a net human and ecological gain or loss; the extreme view was put to me by the kind of traveller whose idea of heaven is unlimited marshy wildfowling country, complete with insects and solitude, and who said, "What a fantastic coast this must have been – before it was improved!"

There is already substantial human gain. The strategically placed blocks of flats, villas and villages, with shrubs and trees, cool and constantly watered, shelter the beaches from the winds that have hitherto kept families in search of relaxation away from this part of the coast; by the time the intensive cultivation of flowers, shrubs and wind-breaks achieves success, the whole aspect of the resorts will be changed. Nothing improves the look of reinforced concrete better than greenery: at Port Leucate the landscape gardening is perhaps (apart from the port and yacht-basin design) the most truly imaginative feature.

Pézenas

Among the inland diversions on the way from Montpellier to Cap d'Agde and Leucate is Pézenas, which lies between the Mediterranean at Agde and the region known as *les Causses* (enclosed by the Cevennes on the east, the valley of the Lot to the north, Rouergue on the west and the plains of the Hérault and the Lower Languedoc to the south). Pézenas, a fortified town under the Romans, became an important market for woollen fabrics, with trading privileges for the merchants who attended the three fairs held there each year. And in 1456 the States General of Languedoc met there for the first time, a tribute to its status which was followed later by the establishment there of the seat of the governors of Languedoc, the Montmorencys and the Contis.

A comfortable small town of just under 10,000 inhabitants, attractively placed amid vineyards, with the coast not more than 12 miles or so away at Cap d'Agde and conveniently situated between Montpellier and Béziers, Pézenas benefits not only from its natural and historic attractions but also from the way these are presented by the local administration and its Syndicat d'Initiative. The S.I., incidentally, is imaginatively installed in what was Barber Gély's shop in the old Marché au Bled, where the playwright Molière, according to tradition, spent hours in the wig-maker's comfortable chairs, listening to and taking part in the customers' conversations.

The Molière connection is one of the greatest attractions of Pézenas, and it is rewarding however much or little the visitor knows of the French dramatist's work. Apart from the charming preservation of Barber Gély's parlour in the S.I., there is the beautiful loggia of the Hôtel d'Alfonce, a gem in itself, like so many of the old houses of Pézenas, and also the setting, it is believed, of the first performance of Molière's *Le Médécin volant* in the presence of the Prince de Conti and his court.

Molière was attracted to Pézenas when Armand de Bourbon, Prince de Conti, then living in the nearby Grange des Prés and surrounded by a court of noblemen, artists and writers, made each session of the Estates General the occasion for a lavish fête, and Molière's company had so much success that the prince gave him the title and privileges of "Actor to the Prince de Conti". The playwright made Barber Gély's house his home when he visited Pézenas and performed regularly not only for the Prince but also in covered-in public squares for the people of the town.

The superb old houses, courtyards and staircases of Pézenas are all clearly but unobtrusively signposted, so that a brief tour is made extremely simple and agreeable: moreover, Pézenas is anything but a mere museum town, and a morning spent in the busy cafés of the Cours Jean-Jaurès (where there is a fine market) alternates pleasantly with wanderings in the medieval and 17th century treasures of the narrow streets. Every summer the "Mirondela dels Arts" is held in the shops, galleries, workrooms and streets, with exhibitions, music, craft demonstrations and general celebrations.

Corbières

One of the most rewarding aspects of Leucate is that it is the nearest coast village to the Corbières. Through the Corbières is one of the most enchanting ways to Carcassonne, but it is more than that: it is also a journey on which to linger, if you can, almost indefinitely. For the Corbières is the kind of region the discriminating traveller would like to keep to himself and a few kindred spirits; the kind of region in which historical and archaeological interest, so-called tourist facilities, transport networks and bargains in folklore fall into place as secondary stimuli compared with the ever-changing charm of the landscape. Mountainous without being grim, bathed in the golden southern light, it is fragrant with herbs and wild flowers.

This region of modest but none the less dramatic mountains and valleys (the highest peak, Bugarach, is about 3700 ft) is bounded by the Pyrenees to the south, the river Aude to west and north, and the Mediterranean (Barcarès–Leucate–Port-la-Nouvelle) to the east. It is one of the most distinctive areas of southern France and is particularly rich in the superbly situated ruins of ancient fortresses which not only recall the Corbières' former role as the Languedoc's last defence against the Roussillon, then Spanish, but are also tragically rich in reminders of the fate of the Cathars in the medieval persecution of religious dissidents.

The richness of the landscape itself, which forms the link between the Massif Central and the Pyrenees, lies in the mixture of magnificently wooded slopes, rugged and thyme-scented moorland, masses of green-broom and thorny gorse, oak and cypress, and mile after mile of vineyards. In the south the gorges of Galamus are full of scenic drama, and in the east, not far from Leucate, is the incredible fortress of Salses, an apparently indestructible mass of rose, ochre and sand-coloured brick and stone, built in 1497. The outer walls are 30 ft thick in parts and equipped with a huge number of firing posts, which made the fortress invulnerable to the short-range cannon-fire of its day. But it is not merely the brooding size and ominous closed face of Salses that creates its unique impression among the most ancient fortresses of France; the sight of its red, russet and ochre walls, towers and great gateway in the Mediterranean light is both beautiful and haunting.

The small town of Salses, incidentally, produces delicious white wines called Macabeu – pronounced *Macabéou*. The heavier red wines of the Corbières are rich in strength and colour, with a bouquet which recalls the herb-scented garrigue; delicious, and a little goes a long way. A wine of more subtlety is the Fitou of this region, and on the western slopes of the main range, near Limoux, is produced a "blanquette de Limoux", a mousseux dessert wine. The Fenouil-lèdes district also has its own bland, friendly wines.

This is the region of splendid châteaux, some in ruins, known as the "sons of Carcassonne". Aguilar, off the D12 from Perpignan, unlike most of its contem-porary strongpoints, is in a very vulnerable position on a rounded hill: all that is left is a polygonal dungeon and the containing wall with six towers. The Château de Queribus, about 11 km (seven miles) south-west of Aguilar (part of the journey must be completed on foot), has been partly restored. It was the last centre of Cathar resistance in 1255, and offers fine views from the terrace of the dungeon. Peyrepertuse, off the D14 which runs from Maury to Rennes-les-Bains (an excellent centre for the Corbières with a modest selection of hotels, pensions and apartments; noted health resort with curative waters), consists of the impressive remains of a majestic château in a splendid position at the summit of a rocky crest. The Col de la Croix brings you within sight of the summit of Bugarach and leads to Soulatge. North of Peyrepertuse is the Château de Termes, once one of the toughest sons of Carcassonne, now in ruins.

What more has the area to offer? The Abbey de Fontfroide, a Cistercian abbey founded at the end of the 11th century (roughly 16 km, 10 miles, north of Aguilar and 13 km, eight miles, south-west of Narbonne), has one of the most beautiful cloisters in southern France. Accessible from the N613 (turn left from the N113 roughly five km from Narbonne on the road to Carcassonne), Fontfroide, which has been in private hands since 1908, has been restored with care and taste and is in a well-kept setting of gardens and walks. Visits are possible during most of the year, beginning on the hour and half-hour, for which there is a moderate charge.

But the charm of the Corbières still lies more in its comparatively unknown corners and villages than in its history-laden relics, though even these have the advantage of having been less trumpeted abroad than the key sites of other areas of the south. Finding the best of the Corbières takes time, but the reward is joy in the region itself. This is particularly true if you are spending your holiday on the nearby coast, which, sun-baked, uncrowded and well provided for as it is, needs to be complemented with the wooded hills, sudden *massifs*, vine-clad valleys and unexpected villages of the hinterland. You will need to explore on the spot to find Treilles, Feuilla, Opoul, Vinegrau, Tautavel and other corners, but they are worth the effort. Leave the N9 (Narbonne to Perpignan) and turn off westwards along the kind of by-roads you thought no longer existed. Take the D12 to Aguilar, and the D611 to the gorges of Fouradad, and then head for Maury by the N117. Queribus and Peyrepertuse will cost you, respectively, a half-hour's climb and an hour and a half – on foot! And do not miss Lagrasse (where the D3 joins the D212), a village built like a strongpoint, with its 12th-century bridge and remains of ramparts, quiet central *place* and old houses. Lagrasse, approximately equidistant between Narbonne and Carcassonne, each roughly 40 km (25 miles) away, enshrines much of the special quality of the Corbières.

Avignon Bridge, Provence

Provence,
Rhône Valley and
the Camargue

Provence

Provence today is largely where you find it. The ancient Roman province, divided into Upper and Lower Provence, with its capital at Aix, includes the following departments: Basses-Alpes, Bouches-du-Rhône, part of the Drôme, the Var and the Vaucluse. Time was when it had its own kings, and later its own counts, and it was finally reunited with France in 1487 under Charles VIII. The French Government Commissariat General dealing with tourism throws a rather wider net, taking in also the Gard Department, the Rhône Valley and the Hautes Alpes. The Regional Committee for Provence–Côte d'Azur, however, limits itself to a wedge with its sharp end at Montelimar and its wide end ranging from Aigues-Mortes to Aix-en-Provence, with the corresponding stretch of coast from Les Stes-Maries-de-la-Mer to Marseilles. And one of the most popular of all guide books concentrates on the Provence of the Rhône, with the addition of those eastern areas of Languedoc which have similar characteristics to those of the Provence of the Rhône.

The poet of Provence, Frédéric Mistral, who died in 1914, took Pont-St-Esprit as the gate through which the Rhône enters Provence. "It is there", he wrote, "that Provence makes its first appearance, where the bridge of St-Esprit curves its twenty superb arches like a crown over the Rhône. It is the sacred portal, the gateway to the Land of Love. The olive, the proud pomegranate and the millet already adorn the slopes and the river valleys. The plain begins to widen, the woodland edge is green in the clear light, and the sky takes on the radiance of Paradise . . ."

Provence is, of course, known as the land of the sun, and this is basically true, compared with northern lands and many other parts of France, even if it is not always and universally true of every corner of Provence at all times. Van Gogh's sun and cypresses are the emblems; vine, olive and lemon are the fruits. The sun is the key, whether on the limestone ranges of Mount Ventoux and the foothills of the Alps, the countryside of Aix, the austere solitude of the heart of the Camargue, the garrigues of Nîmes or the interplay of land and water in the Rhône delta. Also integral to the region is the *mistral*, a wind which comes bellowing down the Rhône valley like a bull, bursts over shipping off the coast with a crack like a gun, dries up the countryside in its path and can do real damage apart from creating, in some areas and among some people, strange tensions and unease. But its imminence and its departure after a few days are both marked by a crystalline clarity in the air, a pristine sharpness of detail in the distance, and a Tiepolo radiance in the sky as if the world had been washed clean.

Montelimar

Perhaps one of the most famous towns of Provence – for its stickily delicious sweetmeat if nothing else – is Montelimar. With about 30,000 inhabitants, it is a splendidly equipped holiday centre, with dozens of hotels and pensions, and every opportunity for sport and recreation, cultural facilities for the young and not-so-young, and easily arranged excursions into the Drôme and the Ardèche – the S.I. is in the Promenade des Allées. It has, too, a wealth of historic buildings and monuments from the 11th century onwards.

It is almost surrounded by highly visitable châteaux, churches, abbeys and beauty spots. The town's name is a corruption of Mount Adhemar, a feudal fortress built there in the 12th century by the Adhemar family, whose last descendant, in the 17th century, was the Comte de Grignan, son-in-law of Mme de Sévigné. During the Wars of Religion Montelimar was besieged and finally taken by the forces of the Reformation. Louis XIII gave the city to the Grimaldis, Princes of Monaco, who held it until the Revolution.

Before continuing the journey south, visit the site of the ruins of Rochemaure, which faces the city across the Rhône. Rochemaure ("black rock") is an area on the right bank of the river where basalt makes a striking contrast with the neighbouring limestone scarps, and is crowned by the ruins of the fortress (dating from the 13th century) and its feudal walled village.

A diversion I would strongly recommend is eastwards into the Drôme round Dieulefit (a heavenly name, to say the least). A round trip from Montelimar by way of La Bégude-de-Mazenc (N540) to Dieulefit, then by the N538 back through Montioux and Rousset to the N541, through Valréas and Grignan to

Donzère, will give you a tempting foretaste of all the Drôme has to offer. Better still, if you have time, take a trip of about 209 km (130 miles) which includes the departmental roads, as well as the national roads, and takes in many attractive stretches of countryside and old villages. Excellent maps and guide-books are available from the Syndicat d'Initiative in Montelimar: one of the most comprehensive on the Drôme as a whole is published by the Comité Départmental du Tourism de La Drôme in Valence. But please send international postal coupons if you want a copy sent to you.

Among the attractions of the area immediately east of Montelimar are Dieulefit itself, with its agreeable climate and beautiful surroundings, the Val des Nymphes and the old village of La Garde-Adhemar, and Grignan, with the château where Mme de Sévigné lived – and which is open to visitors.

From Montelimar the way south towards Orange offers the choice nowadays of using the A7 autoroute (à *péage* over large stretches, which means that you pay a toll), or the "old" N7. Or, better still, by a mixture of the departmental roads and the N7, to say nothing of the scenic advantages of going part of the way along the N86, along the right or west bank of the Rhône.

One recommended route begins by taking the D11 across the Rhône to Rochemaure, where the château is worth a visit. Then follow the N86 south by way of Viviers to the Défilé de Donzère. Then return across the Rhône to take the minor road that runs south between the Rhône itself and the canal that serves Châteauneuf. Where the N540 crosses this minor road, turn left towards Montelimar and then, almost immediately, resume the minor road south. Follow this road (now the D237) to Châteauneuf-du-Rhône, and there pick up the D73 towards Viviers and the Défilé de Donzère, where the two bridges which cross the Rhône upstream and downstream of the Défilé offer splendid views. (Cross the bridges on foot.) Back on the left or east bank of the Rhône pick up the N541 and continue south, breaking off to visit La Garde-Adhemar and the Val des Nymphes; a further detour to Clansayes, with its magnificent views, is highly recommended. Visit the great barrage works at Donzère-Mondragon if you have time, otherwise from Clansayes drive to St-Paul-Trois-Châteaux (D571–D113) and from St-Paul take the D59 to Suze-la-Rousse and D117, D11 and finally N7 to Orange.

Orange

If you enter Orange by the N7 you come almost immediately upon one of the city's two most impressive Roman monuments, the great commemorative or triumphal arch celebrating the exploits of Caesar's 11th Legion and their victory over the Massaliotes, the Greeks who colonised Marseilles, in 49 BC. The survivors of the Legion became the first colonists of Orange, then called Arausio. The other magnificent memorial of the Romans is the finest and best-preserved Roman theatre in Provence – perhaps in the world – situated on the other side of the city, where you pass it before you resume your journey south.

Today the equivalent of a modest county capital, Orange grew during the early centuries of the Christian era from a Celtic settlement or township to become a Roman colony of such importance and prosperity that it had at one period a population far greater than it has today. But this prosperity tempted fate and brought terrible setbacks. In the year 105 BC, Cimbrian and Teton "barbarians", terrifying in sheer size and awe-inspiring in voice to the Romans, launched an attack with such success that 100,000 Romans were left dead. Within three years the Roman general Marius inflicted an even more crushing defeat on the Germanic hordes before Aix, in a triumph which gave its name to the Montagne Ste-Victoire – and also gave Marius's name to large numbers of Provençal boys, to say nothing of Marseilles' favourite figure in comic papers.

A principality in the 13th century, Arausio-Orange came, through marriages and inheritance, into the possession of a branch of the des Baux family and of the German principality of Nassau. In the 16th century William the Silent (William of Nassau, Prince of Orange) created the United Provinces, and the royal dynasty of Holland adopted the title of Orange. Thus the House of Orange-Nassau, while governing the Low Countries (and, for a time, England), also cherished its tiny corner of France. Louis XIV, however, put a stop to all that and handed Orange over to the Comte de Grignan, son-in-law of Mme de Sévigné and Lieutenant-General of Provence.

The commemorative arch, which we saw briefly on the way into Orange, is one of the finest the Romans have left us. The theatre, built during the Augustan era, has, as "backcloth" to the spectacles presented there, what Louis XVI called "the finest wall in the kingdom" – 103 metres long by 38 metres high – from which only the roof and ornamental details of statues and columns are missing. The stepped semi-circle of the auditorium was built into a hillside, which made the construction quicker and cheaper than that of the Roman theatre at Arles. Near the theatre are the ruins of the Capitol and the open space of the Colline St-Eutrope, from which the site of other important Roman remains can be traced. Productions are staged in the Roman theatre at the end of July – details from the Syndicat d'Initiative, Place des Frères Mounet, but please enclose reply coupons.

The S.I. will also send you a thoroughly reliable hotel list, with up-to-date information about the three-star Arène, Terminus and Princes, as well as the inexpensive hotels of the Avenue Frédéric Mistral such as the Français, the Globe, or the Hôtel de la Gare, and the one-star Hôtel des Arts or Le Milan.

Avignon

From Orange the N7 runs south more or less parallel to the A7 autoroute for about 18 km (11 miles) and then passes over it to reach Avignon, making a total of 27 km (17 miles) from Orange. Arriving at Avignon by the N7, it is a good beginning to turn right and follow the old ramparts along the Rhône quays for an introductory glimpse of the famous broken bridge – the Pont d'Avignon, or, to give its correct title, the Pont St-Bénézet. Then I should suggest a visit to the four-star Syndicat d'Initiative, 41, Cours Jean-Jaures, where you will be given every help to make the most of your visit. Don't forget that, in the peak holiday period (July and August), Avignon, which already has a permanent population of about 100,000, attracts enormous numbers of tourists, not only for its scenic and historic attractions, but also for the annual drama and arts festival, so that you are likely to find even the city's ample hotel resources under heavy strain, and the streets crowded.

It is worth while crossing the Rhône by the N100 to Villeneuve-les-Avignon and Les Anglès, where there are a dozen or so hotels. If you decide to do this from the Quai du Rhône south of the Pont St-Bénézet you will have to negotiate a half-clover-leaf junction to reach the N100 bridge – be careful you don't spend part of your holiday driving round an endless loop! Villeneuve-les-Avignon and Les Anglès, with their old corners and fine views, are interesting to stay in: from some of the terraces the sight of a storm gathering in the Rhône valley, and the first breath of the wind, are indeed dramatic.

The Palais des Papes is probably the major historic attraction of Avignon. This massive example of medieval civil and military architecture was built in the 14th century for the Popes Benedict XII and Clement VI. The great walls, with their eight towers, enclose the Clementine Chapel, built over the Great Audience Chamber, two chapels with 14th century Italian frescoes, Clement VI's chamber, and many other items of architectural and historic interest. Next to the great Palais is the 12th-century Cathedral of Notre Dame de Doms and the Petit Palais. Conducted tours are held with varying frequency according to season: from July 1 to September 30 they start every half-hour, morning and afternoon. A moderate charge is made for admission. Some parts of the palace, including Benedict XII's chapel, now in use as a departmental records office, can be visited only if permission is applied for in advance.

The Avignon Drama Festival, founded originally by the late Jean Vilar, who created the National People's Theatre in France, is no longer confined to the art of the theatre, but now includes classical and experimental music, ballet and films. The setting, in the great courtyard of the Palais des Papes, is magnificent, but it is not easy to find seats if you have not booked well in advance. With or without the festival, there is much of historic interest and charm in the city itself.

There is, of course, no lack of appropriate accommodation, from the four-star hotels d'Europe, Les Frênes and Sofitel, through a wide range of medium-priced establishments, down to dozens of small, unpretentious but adequate establishments. None the less, you may well have difficulty in finding somewhere to stay in the high season if you haven't made arrangements in advance.

Avignon is ideally situated on the Rhône in the heart of the Vaucluse Department, which is itself one of the most characteristic areas of Provence. This means that almost every route suggested has attractive variants, and that there are times when it is worth while reducing the time spent in towns and villages, however charming, for the sake of spending more time on the roads that link them.

For example, instead of driving direct from Orange to Avignon one might well – time, money, volume of traffic and family tensions permitting – make a fairly extensive detour (N575) to Vaison-la-Romaine, one of the key sites for Roman antiquities in Provence as well as being an attractively situated medieval town and holiday resort. From Vaison the N538 (turn left at Malaucene on to the N574) offers a magnificent scenic drive in the Mt Serein section of Mont Ventoux, with a further network of beautiful country taking you towards Avignon by way of Carpentras, which is in itself worth a protracted visit.

Carpentras is a lively country town with a history which adds interest and charm rather than mere weight. It has undergone many changes, many of them for the better. Once the centre of a region that was comparatively barren, the immediate countryside was transformed by the diversion of part of the Durance, in the form of the Carpentras canal, into an area of fruit crops and market gardens, dominated on the skyline by Mount Ventoux and the Dentelles de Montmirail. It was the capital of the Comtat Venaissin – territory belonging to the Holy See – from 1320 to the French Revolution, and might well have become the seat of the Papal Palace during the schism which drove the Popes temporarily from Rome, if Pope John XXII had not preferred Avignon. It was also the centre of an important Jewish community in the 16th and 17th centuries, and it was in Carpentras that Henri Fabre, the great French entomologist, taught for several years in the 19th century. It is also celebrated for its *berlingots* – a special kind of boiled sweet which is a regional speciality in many parts of southern France. A charming touch is that its three-star Syndicat d'Initiative is in the Maison du Tourisme et des Vins, Place du Théâtre.

Points of particular interest include the ancient Cathedral of St Siffrein, with its flamboyant Gothic and somewhat mysterious Porte Juive, or Door of the Jews; the synagogue itself, which is the oldest in France, and is all that remains of a ghetto once occupied by 1200 Jews; a Roman arch believed to be coeval with that of Orange; and fragments of the town's original ramparts.

Carpentras holds a summer festival jointly with Vaison-la-Romaine from July 15 to August 15 and there is a service of excursions into the region.

The Way to Arles

After Carpentras the direct route south is by the N542 back to Avignon, and then to Arles, perhaps with digressions to Tarascon (brief) and Les Baux (more leisurely). If, however, you have a taste for mountain roads and hairpin bends with splendid views I recommend the D4 over the Col de Murs to visit the splendidly sited ochre-producing town of Apt. Then drive south on the N543 for 12 km (eight miles) where you turn right (west) on to the winding D36 for about three km. Look out for a forest road on the left. This runs over the Massif des Cedres for 28 km (17 miles) with really breathtaking views of Cavaillon, one of Provence's great melon centres, and thence by the N99 towards Les Baux and Arles. About 120 km (75 miles) from Carpentras to Arles by this detour. A third possibility is to take the N538 due south from Carpentras to l'Isle-sur-la-Sorgue, with a detour to the Fontaine de Vaucluse, then continue along the N538 to Cavaillon. Leave Cavaillon by the N538, and continue westwards to Les Baux, then south to Arles.

This third route, a reasonable compromise, covers about 70 km (43 miles). Six km south of Carpentras is Pernes-les-Fontaines, which was, in fact, the capital of the Comtat Venaissin from 968 to 1320 – that is, before Carpentras. It is a typical township of Vaucluse, busy largely with growing and preserving cherries, strawberries, melons and grapes for the market. It has a Syndicat d'Initiative at Pont de la Nesque, on the bank of the River Nesque on your left as you enter Pernes-les-Fontaines from Carpentras by the N538. A pleasant place to linger in, with a splendid 17th century fountain and a fine old bridge over the Nesque near Notre Dame de Nazareth and two gates that were part of the original containing wall. Hotel accommodation is very limited, but the S.I. has details of rooms and apartments to rent.

About 10 km south along the N538, turn left into the D25 to the Fontaine de Vaucluse (seven km). This is really a spring, or even a winter diversion, since it loses some of its interest when the water-level is low. The fountain itself, one of the most powerful resurgences of underground water in the world, is the reappearance above-ground of an important subterranean river fed by the rainfall on the plateau of Vaucluse and Mount Ventoux. Try to time your visit towards the end of the afternoon, when the sun is on the cliffs. The 14th century Italian poet Petrarch, who lived for 13 years in the Vaucluse, is closely associated with the site.

From the Fontaine de Vaucluse rejoin the N538 and turn left into l'Isle-sur-la-Sorgue, a town enclosed within two arms of the River Sorgue, with an interesting church and Hôtel-Dieu (hospital) containing rich decoration of the 17th and 18th centuries. The Syndicat d'Initiative is close by the church. The 17th century pharmacy has some fine Moustiers pottery, and the charm of the little town, with its avenues of great plane trees, is enhanced by remains of Renaissance houses and some 17th century *hôtels particuliers* (private houses). Originally a village of fishermen, its inhabitants further improved their well-watered site by cutting canals between the arms of the Sorgue. The village has been described as "the Venice of Vaucluse".

Cavaillon, 10 km south of l'Isle-sur-la-Sorgue, with about 19,000 inhabitants, is as firmly associated with the fragrance of melons as Collioure is with ancho-vies, but, on the whole, more agreeably, unless you are a passionate anchovy-fan. The Romans established a trading centre on the fertile plain close to the confluence of the Durance and Coulon rivers, and served by the main routes between Arles and Italy. This became the prosperous town of Cabellion. It was laid waste by barbarian invaders, but rose again so successfully from the ashes as to become a bishopric of some importance up to the French Revolution.

The 12th century cathedral of Notre Dame et St-Véran has a fine apse and gilded 17th century carvings framing a number of pictures. The small 17th century synagogue contains elegant Louis XV woodwork and a noteworthy wrought-iron balustrade round the minister's reading desk. The synagogue and a collection of Jewish historical relics in the basement are open to the public. There is a small charge for admission. There is also a museum of local archaeological finds. The two-star Syndicat d'Initiative is in the Place de la Gare.

At the junction of the Place du Clos and the Place François-Tourel there is a small, finely decorated Roman arch which was found more or less hidden behind the cathedral and transferred to its present site stone by stone in 1880. Here also begins (to the left of the Roman arch) Cavaillon's most popular little outing, by footpath to the Chapelle St-Jacques, with magnificent views on the way. The trip, there and back, takes about three-quarters of an hour: visitors who are not so young or sure-footed need to take reasonable care on the way down to the Place François-Tourel. On the plateau by the chapel are Gallo-Greek remains.

St-Rémy-de-Provence

Leave Cavaillon in a south-west direction by the Avenue du Pont (N538), which crosses first the River Durance then the A7 autoroute, to Plan d'Orgon (fine views), where the road becomes N99 and leads through magnificent country to St-Rémy-de-Provence 17 km (10 miles) away. This township of about 7000 inhabitants is one of the richest treasure-stores of Roman remains in Provence. Originally founded as the settlement of Glanon by the Greeks of Marseilles in the 2nd century BC, the town was taken by Caesar in the year 49 and re-named Glanum. Laid waste by barbarian invaders, it revived to become the scene of a legendary miracle performed by the Bishop of Reims in the year 500, or thereabouts, which gave the town its present name.

The plateau of Les Antiques, as they are known, is one km south of St-Remy, and is crossed by the D5. The Mausoleum and the remains of the Municipal Arch are among the most important Roman relics, while, for the serious student of archaeology, the site of Glanum, with its fragments of walls and columned roadways, is of enormous interest. Work on the site, which began in 1921, is understood to have brought to light so far no more than a tenth of the town, which is believed to have had up to 5000 inhabitants. For a detailed guide to the Roman remains and the excavations, consult the Syndicat d'Initiative, in the south-east corner of the Place de la République. St-Rémy is also reputed to have been the birthplace of Nostrodamus, the 16th century astrologer. There is a reasonable range of hotels and apartments available: the population goes up to at least 10,000 in the peak season.

The leading hotels are the Château des Alpilles and the Hostellerie du Vallon-de-Valrugues, followed closely by the Hôtel des Antiques, Le Castellet, the Cheval Blanc and about a round dozen of smaller places with anything from 18 down to seven rooms.

Les Baux

Go west out of St-Rémy-de-Provence, along the tree-lined Avenue Fauconnet, as far as the hospital, where you take the left fork (D31), a minor road, for about three km, or a little less, to where the D27 crosses the D31. Turn left along the D27 mountain road until the 27a forks off left, and follow this road to Les Baux.

There is much to be said about Les Baux, but nothing the tourist is told about it can equal the first impact of this amazing citadel itself, part natural, part the work of prehistoric man, part due to the kind of rock sculpture carried out by geological and meteorological forces such as we have already seen at work in the "natural ruins" of sites like Montpellier-le-Vieux. The more out of season your visit, of course, the greater the impact, but even in season the crowds and souvenir shops cannot diminish the strangeness and the power of the site.

A mere recital of its historic associations reads like a lunatic costume-film scenario as it might have been put forward by a Hollywood mogul of the early years of the industry. Cave-dwellers and Courts of Love, noble families with titles like Orange, Grimaldi and Les Baux to conjure with; medieval splendour, squalor and brutality, powerful princesses as well as cruel lords; links with Italy and Spain and one of the Magi, King Balthasar . . . All these and the torchlit Christmas shepherds' mass which still goes on would have to be taken into account.

Les Baux is a remarkable human settlement of undetermined antiquity which has retained over the centuries a mystery whose origins are no longer decipherable. Beginning with primeval rock shelters and dwellings first hollowed out of, then built into, the rocks, the village consists of the remains of an ancient fortified castle and some old, dead houses on a rocky plateau on the top of a bare spur of the *Alpilles* or little Alps of Provence, the spur being 220 metres high, 900 metres long and 200 metres wide. From the Charloun Rieu monument at the southernmost tip of the spur, the view extends to Montmajour, Arles, the Crau and the Camargue: on very clear days it is possible to pick out Aigues-Mortes and Les Saintes-Maries-de-la-Mer. To the west is the valley of the Fountain, north-west the Vale of Hell, and to the east and north-east, below the escarpment, rolling country sprinkled with white rocks and boulders that in certain lights look like scattered sheep.

Within the village on the plateau (it has something like 300 inhabitants and a Syndicat d'Initiative) there are the remains of the 17th century Hôtel de Ville, with three vaulted rooms, the gateway that was once the only entrance to Les Baux, a tiny village square, and the remains of a 16th century Protestant temple, as well as the church of St Vincent. There are also several ancient communal baking ovens for the villagers' bread and a fascinating narrow lane, the Rue du Treneat, which has been hollowed out of the rock and further carved into odd shapes by the wind and the rain. The monument at the southern tip of the plateau, which commands such a superb panorama, is of Charloun Rieu, a Provençal poet.

In the Vallon de la Fontaine, below the village of Les Baux, is a charming small Renaissance building, the Pavillon de la Reine Jeanne. Permission to visit it should be sought at the adjoining farm. To get the full flavour of the site Les Baux should, ideally, be visited by moonlight, out of the tourist season. But the torchlight procession of the shepherds' mass is a beautiful spectacle that nothing can spoil: it is not, however, the exclusive prerogative of Les Baux, being common to many of the villages of the Rhône delta and the stony stretch called the Crau. The sixteen-point star which the Lords of Les Baux incorporated in their armorial devices is popularly associated with King Balthasar; but it is also the emblem of the Camargue gipsies, who brought it from the East. In the valley below Les Baux is one of the most celebrated hotels (and restaurants) in France, the Oustau de Baumanière, where Queen Elizabeth II stayed during a holiday. There is also the Hostellerie de la Reine Jeanne in the village itself, while in the valley are several more establishments, including La Ribolo de Taven, La Cabro d'Or, Le Mas d'Aigret and La Benvengudo.

Tarascon and Beaucaire

Within easy reach of Les Baux are Tarascon and Beaucaire, on the left and right banks of the Rhône respectively. Tarascon has been associated for 2000 years with a legendary amphibious monster, the Tarasque, whose habit of feeding on the inhabitants of the Rhône valley was checked only when Ste Martha (who had accompanied Les Saintes Maries to Provence from Palestine) sprinkled holy water on it so that it became docile and allowed the local people to cut it into pieces. Tarascon is also familiar to English students of French from the novels and short stories of Alphonse Daudet. The mill from which he wrote his "Lettres de mon moulin" is not far from the town.

There is always talk of reviving the picturesque processions with which the taming of the Tarasque used to be celebrated: the Syndicat d'Initiative, in the

The great stalagmite, Aven Armand grotto

La Grande Motte, Languedoc

Place du Château, will have full details, along with information about the festivals in honour of Tartarin, the character created by Alphonse Daudet in his novels who has become as much a part of the lore of Tarascon as the Tarasque itself. But Tarascon has other rewarding aspects, apart from legends and 19th century French literature. The great 12th century château on the bank of the Rhône is undoubtedly one of the finest feudal castles in France and its terraces offer views that should not be missed. There are conducted tours at set times, according to the season. The week-day admission fee is halved on Sundays and holidays.

The château of Beaucaire faces that of Tarascon from the other side of the Rhône. The enormous international fair which made Beaucaire famous throughout Europe from the 13th century until comparatively recently has left little trace except in so far as the town is still a busy and lively river-port for wine, and this is enhanced by the fact that the canal from the Rhône to Sète runs along the south side of the town, flanked by the tree-lined Quai du Général-de-Gaulle and the Cours Gambetta. The two-star S.I. in the Hôtel de Ville (Place Clemenceau) has an impressive list of houses and public buildings worth seeing in the town and its surroundings. The holiday attractions of Beaucaire are indicated by the fact that the population goes up from the normal 13,000 to well over 15,000 in the high summer.

Arles

Back to Tarascon, and southbound by the N570 to Arles, 19 km (12 miles), one of the capital cities of Roman France, gateway to the Camargue and city of the arts, closely associated with literature (Frédéric Mistral and Alphonse Daudet), music (Gounod and Bizet), and painting (Van Gogh).

Arles is essentially a city where you should begin your visit by getting to know the Syndicat d'Initiative, the three-star office of tourist information in the Palais de l'Archevêché, 35, Place de la République. There are so many conducted and lecture tours available, so many local excursions possible throughout the year, and so many trips for visitors with specialised interests that you will find it well worth while weighing up the alternatives and making your choice before you become exhausted by unsystematic ramblings. There is an excellent selection of hotels, from the four-star Jules Cesar and a dozen three-star establishments to a number of more modest, but comfortable establishments without restaurants; here again, consult the lists at the Syndicat d'Initiative, which, while never recommending any particular establishment rather than another in the same price range, guarantees by the inclusion of hotels in its list that they have been checked to see that they fulfil the requirements of French law relating to such establishments.

The town has grown up astride a narrowish stretch of the main arm of the Rhône, the Grand Rhône, which widens appreciably south of Arles and flows in broad splendour to the Mediterranean just beyond Port St-Louis. The other arm of the river, the Little Rhône, branches off westwards just north of Arles and then winds its way south to the Mediterranean near Les Stes-Maries-de-la-Mer, forming the western boundary of the Camargue. But the situation of Arles was not always like this. The area we call the Bouches du Rhône was once a vast estuary with a few rocky islands, of which the island of Arles was one. In time the estuary became more and more silted up with the material brought down by the Rhône, creating the complex of marshland, sandbanks, lagoons, islets, and salt-flats we know today.

Even more interesting than the changes in the physical setting of the town were the later changes in its status in occupied Gaul, when, from being a dependency of Marseilles, Arles supplanted it as the chief port. When Marseilles took sides with Pompey against Caesar, Caesar ordered Arles to build him a fleet strong enough to bring the colonists of Marsielles to heel. The fleet, according to some accounts, was delivered to him within a month. Arles was rewarded with the spoils of Marseilles, and became the great sea- and river-port of the Gauls, growing century by century until the Emperor Constantine took up imperial residence there, and his successors made it the capital city of the Gauls.

Roman Arles consisted of a fortified town on the left bank of the Rhône entirely enclosed by a wall with four gates flanked by towers, and a residential district of substantial villas on the right bank. The two halves of the town were linked by a bridge of boats. In its Roman heyday it must have been one of the wonder-cities of the world, with an amphitheatre that could hold the entire population of the town, a 16,000-seat theatre, a circus, a basilica, triumphal arches here and there to remind the populace of the power of Rome, and baths as big as those of Caracalla in Rome. As a fair amount of this splendour has survived, there is a great deal for the visitor to see.

Ideally you might begin your visit by arming yourself with a good street-plan in which the principal sights are clearly marked and, starting from the Boulevard des Lices (site of the ancient "lists" or tiltyard where tournaments were held), see as many of the important sights as possible, making note of those which attract you most, so that, if you have the time, you can return to them with fuller information from the S.I. In this way you can eliminate all those objects in which you cannot really become interested except with a positive effort of will – or a sense of duty, which has no place on a holiday trip. The tour will include, of course, the amphitheatre, the Roman theatre, the church of St Trophime and the Alyscamps (ancient burial-ground painted many times by Van Gogh), which you should visit after your tour of the centre of the town.

Do not, in any case, miss the Arlaten Museum – or Museon Arlaten, to give it its Provençal title. This was created in 1897 by the Provençal poet Frédéric Mistral, who also contributed towards its maintenance the entire sum of the Nobel Prize which was awarded to him in 1904. The collection, which is displayed in a 16th century private mansion – l'Hôtel de Castellane-Laval – gives a comprehensive survey of the costume, arts, crafts, popular art, trades, music and folk-lore of the region. There is also a permanent collection of Picasso drawings in the Reattu Museum, as well as an exceptionally fine collection of work by the master-photographers of our time, the world's second most important collection of Paleo-Christian art in the Museum of Christian Art, and an impressive Museum of Pagan Art.

Attractions of a different kind include festivals, bull-running in the streets, cinemas, music, theatre, and the extensive range of Provençal food and wines, with local emphasis on dishes prepared with Camargue rice and the celebrated smoked sausage of Arles. Best of all, since this is the south, sit in the sun (or the shade) in the Boulevard des Lices or the public gardens, or by the

Rhône, or in the Place de la République, or in a café under the trees, and read about the places you will visit when the sun goes in.

Nyons

An alternative to coming south down the Rhône valley is to run a little farther east of the river and, on leaving the Drôme, make your way to Toulon by way of Nyons, Mount Ventoux, Lourmarin, Pertuis and Aix-en-Provence. For this route, continue south from Dieulefit along the N538 to Nyons, where the Nîmes–Gap route (N94) crosses the N538 – in itself a pleasant alternative to the N7 or the autoroute.

Nyons is a pleasant small town (about 4500 population) with an agreeable climate all the year round and an attractive quality in the light. Although it has, in the main, attracted retired people and others who value the mildness of its winter climate, it has more than enough interest to justify a two-star Syndicat d'Initiative, in the Place de la Liberation, and there is a reasonable choice of hotels and apartments in or near the town. In fact, the lack of world-famous monuments makes it all the easier to enjoy the quiet old district (the Quartier des Forts) and the hump-back, 15th century bridge over the River Eygues (or Aygues, as you still occasionally find it spelt). The Place du Dr-Bourdongle is arcaded, as all good squares should be. There is a pleasant eight km walk or drive to the north-west of the town known as the Promenade Anglais et de Vaulx.

Sheltered by the surrounding hills, rich in exotic plants, in the midst of olive groves and orchards, Nyons' specialities include truffles, fresh and preserved fruit, lavender, and Haut-Comtat wines. It is situated between the Tricastin plain and the mountains of La Lance and Veyronne, and you could do much worse than make it a base for leisurely trips into the Baronnies, the Montagne de Bluye and Mount Ventoux itself.

From Nyons and Mount Ventoux head south-east through the Venaissin to the gorges of La Nesque and to Sault (N542), then by N543 south over the Plateau de Vaucluse to join the N100 just under two km west of Apt: turn left into the town. (Nyons to Apt – check with the S.I. for the best and most practicable scenic route according to the time of year.)

Apt is a sizeable place for a town known as the "capital of crystallised fruits", with a permanent population of something like 15,000, and a Syndicat d'Initiative in the Pavillon du Tourisme, Place de la Bouquerie. It is a busy centre – the major source of ochre in France – with tree-lined walks along the bank of the Coulon, ramparts, and the first sanctuary dedicated to Ste-Anne in France, the Basilica-Cathedral of Ste-Anne, built in the late 11th or early 12th century. It is a centre for fine drives into the Luberon, the so-called "Colorado of Provence", the Fontaine de Vaucluse and to many quiet mountain villages. A 23 km (14 miles) round trip from Apt (D113) takes you to the ancient Fort de Buoux and the remains of the priory of St Symphorien. Route details and advice from the S.I.

Alternatively this trip could be incorporated in the next stage of your journey south by the N543 over the Luberon to Lourmarin and Cadenet. Lourmarin (two small hotels and a pension), 19 km (12 miles) south of Apt, is associated with Albert Camus, the Nobel Prize-winning French novelist, who died in 1960 and is buried in the village cemetery. The château is worth a visit (a few francs for a half-hour guided tour), and the birthplace of Philippe de Girard, who invented a flax-spinning machine in the 19th century, is now a museum which can be visited for a small charge. The Luberon mountain itself, divided by the N543 into the Grand Luberon on the east and the Petit Luberon on the west, is full of interest, scenic and historic. There are many picturesquely situated villages and the area is noteworthy for the number of dry-stone huts known as "bories" or "borrys", some of considerable antiquity which appear to have been used not only as shelters or shepherds' bothies, but also as primitive homes. It was on the southern slopes of the Luberon that the followers of Pierre Valdo, who became known as "Vaudois", practised their "heresy" of simplified, reformed evangelism and were put to death or driven from their land.

Cadenet, just under five km farther south, has, in the main square, the statue of a young drummer-boy, the "Tambour d'Arcole". This commemorates André Etienne, born in Cadenet, who, during Bonaparte's fierce battle with the Austrians at the Pont d'Arcole, in Italy, in November 1796, swam across the river and beat the "charge" from the other side. The Austrians, fearing that they were between two fires, retreated.

Aix-en-Provence

From Cadenet continue south along the N553, crossing the Durance and the N561, until you join the N7, when you turn left to Aix-en-Provence, just under 30 km (19 miles) from Cadenet.

Aix, as befits the ancient capital of Provence, with a permanent population of 100,000 – and heaven knows how many more visiting or merely passing through the town in peak season – a world-famous international music festival in July, and a great deal of 17th and 18th century character and charm, has a four-star Syndicat d'Initiative, in the Place du Général de Gaulle. This is open in the season from 08.00 to 23.00; on Sundays and holidays it opens from 08.30 to 12.30 and from 18.00 to 23.00. Out of season it is open from 08.00 to 19.00 and on Sundays and holidays from 08.30 to 12.30.

It has at least 30 good hotels with restaurants, ranging from the four-star Le Roy René, Le Mas d'Entremont, Paul Cezanne, and Le Pigeonnet, through all grades down to modest but adequate no-star establishments, and 30 to 40 other hotels without restuarants, to say nothing of other accommodation in and near the town, with camping and caravan sites within easy reach. But if you are making a last-minute, unprepared dash by car to the Côte d'Azur from the north, do not assume that you will be able to pull up in Aix on your final lap and find just the accommodation you want at the price you want to pay. You might be lucky, but it is better to make sure in advance, or make your stop elsewhere.

Historically and culturally, Aix is one of the most interesting towns in France. So rich, indeed, is its background that any visitor spending more than a few days there might well find the pleasure of the holiday enhanced by a little digging into some corners of the past. There is, of course, the story of the Roman general Marius, whose crushing defeat of the Teutonic invaders in 102 BC is said to be the origin of the name of the Montagne Ste-Victoire. A period of greater interest, from the point of view of the more positive arts of peace, was the reign of the monarch still known as the Good King René. The Counts of Provence had, since the 12th century, made the Court at Aix a centre of cultural and literary refinement, a process which reached its point of highest development in the 15th century under King René. René, Duke of Anjou, titular King of Sicily and Count of Provence, was a classical scholar who was also familiar with the Hebrew and Catalan tongues. He was a skilled musician, both composer and executant, painted, wrote poetry, and was a student of the sciences as well as law. He introduced the muscat grape into Provence and encouraged popular festivals with the object of preserving ancient folk-lore and the traditions of chivalry. The Court over which he presided was one of the most cultivated Europe has known.

In the 18th century Aix knew the incredible Count Mirabeau, whose extraordinary career culminated in his turning his back on his peers in 1789 and getting himself elected as a representative of the Third Estate – the people.

Even today, crowded and bustling, car-packed and, at times, noisy, Aix still retains much of its 18th century elegance, with many of the sober, dignified great houses of the period still a pleasure to the eye. Splendid tree-lined avenues – the Cours Mirabeau is superb – fountains, walks, old corners, quiet squares and, to add to the pleasure of your walks or your placid pauses under the trees, there are always the delicious *calissons* – the almond-flavoured sweets which are as much a part of Aix as the Cours Mirabeau itself. At Palette, near Aix, they serve a wine which goes particularly well with the local sweets and confectionary.

On a more serious level, Aix not only offers the excellent wines of the Coteaux d'Aix, but also harks back to its Roman days, when it was called Aquae Sextiae, in providing curative waters of all kinds in its thermal establishments which offer relief from a great variety of ailments.

With its carnival season from June to the beginning of September, its July music festival, the activities of the students of its university faculties of law and literature (all that is left to Aix of a great university founded in the 15th century), and its favoured situation at the heart of Provence, it is an ideal centre for excursions, exploration, study or sheer relaxation.

The Camargue

The Camargue is an area of 56,000 hectares (roughly 140,000 acres) of alluvial deposit and salt-marshes between the two arms of the Rhône extending from just north of Arles, where the river divides, to the sea. Between the vast Étang de Vaccarès (about 15,000 acres) at its heart, and the sea, is what can only be described as a watery desert of salt-marshes, dunes, pools, lagoons, *étangs*, partially enclosed by long, sweeping sandbanks and constituting an area 'twixt wind and water which only the expert can safely negotiate. An area of about 27,000 acres, with the Étang de Vaccarès as its centre, is now a national zoological and botanical reserve open only to bona fide naturalists and other scientific workers, who must apply, well in advance, to the Conservateur de la Réserve, M. J. de Caffarelli, 2, rue Honore-Nicolas, Arles, for permission to visit the area.

The traditional Camargue, waterlogged and salt-impregnated, is, nevertheless, anything but a sterile wasteland or a vast romantic solitude, but the cultivation of its resources has demanded an unremitting struggle. Drainage, desalination and irrigation with fresh water go on continuously, and throughout the northern part of the Camargue, vine, rice and other cereals are cultivated; the abundant water and the climate have enabled the rice crop (originally grown to prepare the land for other crops) to exceed in yield per acre the production of tropical rice countries.

Much of the traditional Camargue, in fact, remains; plants that thrive on salt feed the herds of wild bulls which still roam the area, while in the Rieges islands, south of the Étang de Vaccarès, spring sees a marvellous display of wild flowers. The bulls, bred for the bull-running and cockade-snatching sports of Provence, are herded by the *gardiens*, with their cowboy hats and trident-goads, who ride the range on their tough Camargue horses, guarding and rounding-up the bulls and the locally bred horses which are said to be of a very ancient breed. And wherever you eat on the fringe of the Camargue you can be sure *boeuf gardien* will be on offer.

Much of the Camargue, like much of the life of the gipsies, has been grossly commercialised and vulgarised to meet what is (largely erroneously) believed to be the univeral tourist taste. But there is still much of interest and beauty and strangeness, and for those who are drawn to areas where land and water are intermingled almost indistinguishably, there is still a magic that no other kind of landscape can convey.

There are three principal ways of visiting the Camargue: one for the holidaymaker dependent on public transport; one for the motorist with the time and interest to look further; and one (already mentioned), for the specialist who will be able to go to the heart of the matter.

A reconnaissance trip by bus from, say, Montpellier is by no means the worst way of getting a glimpse of the Camargue. These excursions run frequently from the middle of July, less frequently during the first fortnight of July, and in June when there is sufficient demand. (This means that you have to inquire at the bus station or at the S.I. and put your name down for the date on which a trip has been provisionally arranged.) The drivers are well informed and helpful, and they give you just the right amount of information to digest at various points. And when the driver points out something it is well worth looking, for he is always the first to spot herds of Camargue bulls and horses, the mounted *gardiens* with their tridents, egrets or a surprisingly large number of other birds, and the picturesque *cabanons* of the *gardiens*. Don't be put off by the sight of pseudo-Wild West ranch-houses with hitching-posts: it is a harmless enough holiday game on the outer fringes of the Camargue, and there is good riding if you have a reliable guide.

The walled town of Aigues Mortes is an astonishing survival, and even Les Stes-Maries-de-la-Mer is not too crowded in the early part of the year. If, as you approach the Camargue proper, the bus driver slips in a cassette of Manitas de Plata and his family singing and playing at a gipsy festival at Arles, it is, after all, one of the best of Manitas's early recordings. But, unless you find the spectacle of wild birds, including flamingoes, mooning around in restricted spaces to be totally irresistible, I suggest you dispense with a visit to the municipal zoo not far from the Mas de Cacherel: better to stay with the coach and watch the marshes for free-roaming bulls or egrets . . .

Alternatively, you have a choice of routes from Arles which will give you a better idea of the Camargue as a whole. You can take the N570 via Albaron to Les Stes-Maries-de-la-Mer, 40 km (25 miles), or, starting on the N570, turn left after about three km and follow the D36 to Port St-Louis. The D36 then turns back to Salin-de-Badon and Villeneuve, whence the D37 takes you to Albaron. About four km before you reach Albaron there is a short cut to the Mas de Cacherel and Les Stes-Maries-de-la-Mer, about 16 km (10 miles), but this is only for the adventurous in very dry weather; it takes you through the heart of the Camargue of the bulls.

Finally, if you can prove that you are qualified to make the best possible use of the visit, you can visit the Étang de Vaccarès, the last stronghold of the wild-life of the old Camargue. This is one of the largest and most important staging-posts in bird migrations between northern Europe and Africa and has been a Mecca for ornithologists for a decade. Serious bird-watchers are welcomed, casual visitors and photographers generally discouraged. Moreover, on a wider scale, farmers, naturalists and the *gardiens* have created a Regional Park in the Camargue under the auspices of the Government, in the hope of exercising local control over the area, rather than being subject to national regulations. But the potential enemies of the Camargue are not confined to hunters, tourists, promoters of dude ranches or vandals indifferent to wild-life: the area is also threatened by unrestricted concrete resort development and land clearance on the one hand, and tremendous industrial development on the other – oil refineries and steelworks and other enterprises.

Aigues-Mortes

But even if you are unable to visit the wild-life reserve itself there is more than enough of human and historical interest elsewhere in the Camargue, with the ever-present possibility of seeing occasional specimens of the rarer birds that use the sanctuary. Of the towns Aigues-Mortes is, to me, by far the most interesting and attractive. Its amazingly well-preserved and sun-baked walls – a complete enceinte of 13th century ramparts with its magnificent Tour de Constance – enclose a small town which has, in spring at least, all the charm of a southern village. It is a holiday resort with a lively centre of shops, restaurants, narrow streets full of character, and little squares, but entirely without the plastic tattiness of small towns on sea-fronts. Aigues-Mortes – Dead Waters – is in fact about four miles from the sea, amid marshes, lagoons and salt-flats. It is both historic (St Louis and the Crusades) and alive; its charm lies as much in its extraordinary completeness today as in the past, and in its uniqueness among walled towns. From the Tour de Constance you can walk round the ramparts in about three-quarters of an hour – an experience not to be missed. The ramparts include twenty towers of various shapes and sizes and ten gates or narrow entries; the total effect is that of a community which, having found a good life, was determined to defend it, rather than the usual medieval impression of a stronghold from which its builder spent all his time looking out for someone to attack.

Les Stes-Maries-de-la-Mer is best known as a place of pilgrimage for the gipsies who are especially devoted to Sara, the black servant who, according to tradition, accompanied Mary Jacoby, sister of the Virgin, and Mary Salome, mother of the Apostles James the Greater and John, when the boat in which they had drifted from Palestine ran ashore near where the Church of the Stes-Maries-de-la-Mer now stands. Having founded a simple place of worship dedicated to the Virgin, the disciples of Christ (in the frail craft were also the resuscitated Lazarus and his sisters Martha and Mary-Magdalen, as well as Maximin and Sidonie) separated. Martha went to preach the gospel in Tarascon, Mary-Magdalen continued her penitence at St-Baume, Lazarus went to preach at Marseilles, Maximin and Sidonie went to Aix. The two Maries and Sara stayed in the Camargue where a rapidly growing cult developed round their remains, which were buried in the simple oratory. The church that replaced the oratory was fortified in the 9th century and incorporated in the ramparts of the town: the present impressive structure dates from the 12th century. Pilgrimages take place in May for Mary Jacoby, and in October for Mary Salome. In May the gipsies gather at the tomb of their patron Sara and the religious ceremonies are followed by days of secular festivities with horse-racing, bull-running, and dancing. Every three or four years, it is believed, the gipsies use this opportunity to elect a new queen.

Chartreuse de la Verne, Collobrières

Côte d'Azur – Marseilles to St-Tropez

The Mediterranean coast from Marseilles to Menton and its immediate hinterland – a region which falls naturally into two parts, Provence–Côte d'Azur from the Bouches-du-Rhône to St-Raphael, and the Riviera–Côte d'Azur from St-Raphael to the Italian frontier – has never been an entirely unalloyed paradise. Even the wealthy pioneers who first nosed it out as a winter retreat had to endure all the hardships of 18th and 19th century travel to get there, as well as the vagaries of an unfamiliar way of life, unfamiliar insects and food and the strange moods and language of the local inhabitants. Even with the coming of the roads and the railways there were still mosquitoes and engine-smoke to contend with up to a quarter of a century ago, and many of us grew up with an image of the Côte d'Azur in which dazzling seas, sunlit mountains, brilliantly flower-decked little railway stations and heart-aching glimpses of lemons or mimosa or olives had to triumph over bouts of choking engine-smoke as the great trains clattered through mountain tunnels on their journey along the coast. The tideless blue Mediterranean has always been polluted to varying degrees by human waste, and some of the most charming of the older hillside residences so much admired today were the forerunners of the building blight which appears likely to leave no acre of land unspoilt.

Marseilles

Just over 40 years ago the French writer of a standard regional guide-book described Marseilles as "admirably situated at the point where the sandy and inhospitable shores of the Lion Gulf meet the rocky cliffs, indented by welcoming bays, of the Côte d'Azur". The shores of the Lion Gulf, which stretch from Marseilles west and south almost to the Pyrenees, are still sandy but no longer inhospitable, with a string of modern, mosquito-free resorts and some of the best-equipped pleasure ports in Europe – perhaps in the world. The Côte d'Azur is still, in spite of everything, an incomparable stretch of rocky coastline deeply indented with marvellous bays, a region of natural beauty which only a geological or nuclear cataclysm could totally destroy.

And at the nodal point stands Marseilles, dividing the *yin* of Languedoc and Roussillon from the *yang* of Provence, the Côte d'Azur and the Riviera. . . . Marseilles, where, it has been suggested with justice, Gaul began, and Africa begins.

Marseilles is the second largest city and first port of France, with one million inhabitants. It also claims to be the most ancient city of France, since its origins go back to the 6th century BC. For many of its visitors, whatever the purpose of their visit, it has always been one of the most dramatic cities of the world, dramatic in its structure, its history, its mixture of threats and promises, its pullulating life and, at times, its enduring mystery. The ideal ways of arriving in Marseilles are still by sea or by rail, by sea for obvious reasons, and by rail because no one who ever arrived for the first time in Marseilles at St Charles Station and walked out on to the terrace that looks across the stone valley of the great city to the Vieux Port, and beyond it to the impressive, lofty mass of Notre Dame de la Garde, is ever likely to forget it.

Like all great ports Marseilles is rich in tall stories and ancient legends, from gross comments on the pollution-content of the Vieux Port to innumerable theories – academic, folk-loric, mythological or simply Gallic – about the name of the district known as "La Belle de Mai". The name of the Canebière itself is said to derive from *chenevières* – hemp plantations. But whereas one explanation is that in the Middle Ages the marshland round the Vieux Port was planted with hemp which was made into rope locally for rigging, another is that the word "chenevière" could just as well refer to a place where hemp was sold, which would naturally be near where the ropemakers worked. Wherever the truth lies, the fact undoubtedly remains that hemp – in some form or other – has always been associated with Marseilles.

And even if the Marseilles of today is no longer the city of Marius, Fanny, Olive, Cesar and Panisse – the city of Pagnol – and the Vieux Port is not what it was, there is still enough of historic, social, civic and artistic interest to satisfy the most demanding traveller.

Start your visit (inevitably) in the Canebière, where at No. 4 you will find the excellent Syndicat d'Initiative combined with the Office Municipal de Tourisme. Here you will find everything you need in the way of help and guidance to see the landmarks of the city's first 25 centuries, from the remains of the ancient Greek and Roman settlements to medieval treasures and such magnificent achievements of later centuries as the lively streets round the Canebière (the rue de Rome and the handsome Avenue du Prado) and the splendid water-front drive of the Corniche President J. F. Kennedy.

Despite the sprawling commerciality of Marseilles there are a number of sights, buildings and museums well worth discovering. You will get an exceptionally good view over the Vieux Port from Pharo Park, a pleasant garden originally belonging to the palace of Empress Eugenie, wife of Napoleon III. The Old Port now largely accommodates only pleasure craft and the surrounding quays and narrow streets are continually alive with strollers, shops and charming little fish restaurants where you will find the traditional dish of Marseilles, *Bouillabaisse*, prepared and eaten with great dedication to the art. The two sturdy forts guarding the harbour entrance are St Jean to the north and St Nicholas (built by Vauban) to the south. Commanding fantastic views across the city is the church of Notre Dame de la Garde, reached only after a steep climb – but worth the effort.

Marseilles has always been associated with the sea and the Roman Docks Museum will give you an excellent idea of the development of the town as a port from ancient times – the Maritime Museum deals with seafaring history from the 17th century to the present. Housed in the Longchamp Palace is the Natural History Museum, which also contains an interesting Aquarium. The Museum of Fine Arts is also located in the palace.

On the south side of the Old Port near to Fort St Nicholas is the fortified Basilica of St Victor built in the 11th century but still housing the original 5th century shrine constructed by St John Cassian. The city's cathedral was built in the 19th century, but in character with so much of Marseilles stands adjacent to the original 12th century building of which only part of the nave and transept remains – a good example of Romanesque architecture. Old Marseilles certainly seems to struggle for existence, but in the Museum of Old Marseilles you will find a unique collection of exhibits portraying everyday life in previous centuries. Another deviation worth making time for is a visit to the Borély Chateau just to the south of the city which houses the Museum of Mediterranean Archaeology; the Egyptian section is a must and the mansion also contains some fine drawings by the 18th century masters including Fragonard, Boucher and Ingres. The tourist office in Canebière will provide you with information on the many excursions on offer to places of interest outside the city.

But for most holidaymakers in France the chief attraction of Marseilles is as the starting point for the Mediterranean coast, going eastwards towards the Riviera proper. There was a time when, using the local trains or the roads, one could make a leisurely journey from the *calanques* or fjords immediately east of Marseilles, by way of Cassis, La Ciotat, Les Lecques, Bandol, Sanary, Hyères, Le Lavandou, Cavalière, Cavalaire and St-Tropez to St-Raphael, before plunging into the traditional Riviera. And there was a time when this trip was rewarded with successive holidays in any of these places – smallish, comparatively unspoiled fishing villages or resorts. Some of them now, alas, have spread all over the place, their populations monstrously swollen during the season, their former charm hidden under massive blocks and commercial developments.

None the less, all is not yet lost. The coast is still incomparable over great stretches, and the hinterland is not yet totally overgrown by buildings and petrol stations. Some of the smaller places have suffered far more than others; some still have the magic of an earlier Mediterranean world.

South through Sisteron

There are two main routes south from Grenoble to the Côte d'Azur between Marseilles and St-Raphael. The N75, with various detours, gives the first full promise of the south once you are over the Col de la Croix-Haute and continues through Sisteron, Peyruis, Forcalquier, Manosque, Brignoles to Toulon. The N85, which forks left from the N75 about 10 km south of Grenoble at le Pont-de-Claix, goes through Gap, Sisteron, Digne, St-André-les-Alpes, Castellane, Draguignan, Le Muy, Fréjus and St-Raphael. There are, of course, many variations, which are best checked on the spot.

Sisteron is reached by way of Aspres-sur-Buech (altitude 762 metres), a mountain village with a natural mineral spring, caves, picturesque ruins, a one-star hotel, le Parc, and a camping site, and of Serres (680 metres), which is a most attractive little town built on the slopes of a rocky promontory overlooking the Buech, a site which has been fortified since the 10th century. Its riches include the splendid old Hôtel de Lesdiguières, a 12th century church, a chapel cut out of the solid rock, some interesting houses of the 14th, 15th and 16th centuries, and the remains of ramparts. There are three hotels, one four-star camping site, and another, more modest, one.

About 30 km (19 miles) farther south and about 200 metres nearer sea-level is Sisteron, a town of approximately 7000 inhabitants, whose population grows to 10,000 and more in the season. Driving in from the north on the N75 you cross the Buech river, which joins the Durance at the north-west corner of the town.

The indispensable Syndicat d'Initiative (two-star) is in Les Arcades, and offers an excellent street-plan, leaflets and other illustrated material. Sisteron, in its rocky setting, occupies a key position at a point where Provence and the old Dauphine meet, and has always been a strongpoint. The impressive citadel, on the summit of a rocky escarpment, still dominates the town and there is a conducted tour with sound effects. A maze of old, vaulted streets leads to the Romanesque cathedral of Notre Dame, and can be conveniently explored by following the wall signs provided by the S.I. In July and August there is a Festival of Music and Drama, held in the Citadel and in the Cloister of St Dominique. The surrounding country is well worth exploring, with excursions to the impressive Rocher de la Baume – the great rock that faces the citadel across the Durance – and to many attractive villages and mountain roads. Trout and game, lamb and *pieds-paquets* (sheep's tripe stuffed with garlic, onions, parsley and pickled pork), nougat, fruit and honey are local specialities.

There are about a dozen hotels, ranging from the three-star Grand Hotel du Cours to a number of modest but adequate places with only a few rooms.

Some of these do not serve meals. A line to the S.I. would bring the latest information, but please don't forget to send an international postal coupon for reply.

From Sisteron continue south to Château-Arnoux, and on leaving the town turn left along the N96 through Peyruis. Between 4 and 5 km beyond Peyruis turn right and follow the D12 to Forcalquier (about 5 km). Forcalquier is a pleasant summer resort with half a dozen hotels, houses and apartments, a number of letting agencies for holiday accommodation, and a useful Syndicat d'Initiative. It has a fair range of entertainment and sport available in the season, and a wide range of excursions is offered. It is an excellent centre for charcuterie and game, as well as mushrooms and truffles and several varieties of goat's-cheese. The 12th century church and medieval houses ensure those quiet sun-baked or shaded corners in which to spend a lazy southern afternoon.

From Forcalquier drive west along the N100 for about 12 km (eight miles), or a little more, until you reach the N207, which turns off to the left. Follow this road to Manosque, at the eastern end of the Luberon massif. Manosque is one of those small southern towns which seem to have had too much history and now lie basking in the sun, content to leave the stage to others. It maintains this relaxed air, strangely enough, in spite of being an important agricultural and trade centre. Enclosed in its fine tree-lined boulevards, which have replaced the ancient ramparts, it offers, in a stroll from the ancient Soubeyran gate to the Saunerie gate, the epitome of a picturesque Provençal town, with its narrow ways and tall houses.

With seven "starred" hotels and an excellent Syndicat d'Initiative in the Place Dr P. Joubert, Manosque is a good centre for exploring the valley of the Durance, for fishing, and for many other sports. It has two industrial zones outside the town, a flying club, and opportunities for good riding. From Manosque I would suggest a leisurely drive south to the sea at Cassis-sur-Mer; the Syndicat d'Initiative would best advise you about the minor roads, according to the time of year. Cassis is the first Mediterranean port-cum-holiday resort east of Marseilles.

South through Gap and Digne

Another route south in this part of the country, the N85 from Grenoble, with variations, runs through Gap, Digne, Castellane and Draguignan to the Mediterranean. Gap, like Sisteron, is on the Route Napoleon, an impressive work of road improvement which was inaugurated in 1932. It marks the route followed by the Emperor on his return from Elba, when he landed at Golfe-Juan and marched to Grenoble. The Syndicats d'Initiative at all stages of the route have adopted eagles in flight as the symbol of the new road project, echoing Napoleon's phrase: "The Eagle will fly from bell-tower to bell-tower until he reaches the towers of Notre Dame . . ."

In fact Gap is mainly a place on the way to somewhere else, though the fact that its population increases in the high season from about 28,000 to 40,000 suggests that it also makes an excellent holiday base.

This indeed is the case, and it has justified the development of a three-star

Syndicat d'Initiative with ample information and advice about such places of interest in the area as the Lac de Serre-Ponçon, the valleys of the Champsaur, the Devoluy, the Valgaudemar and the Queyras, and many lovely drives over mountain passes (Gap itself stands at 735 metres, that is, 2461 ft). There are about 30 hotels in and around the town (though this includes some very small ones), a fair amount of other accommodation and excellent camping sites.

Until the end of the 17th century Gap still retained traces of its long history as a fortress town (Vapincum), but in 1692 a great fire destroyed almost 800 of its 953 dwellings. It is still, however, capital of the Hautes-Alpes Department and an important commercial centre, and has an impressive Romanesque–Gothic cathedral. The winter-sports resorts of Superdevoluy, Ceuse, Orcières-Merlette and Ancelle are within easy reach.

Follow the Route Napoleon (N85) in the reverse direction to Napoleon, through Sisteron to Château-Arnoux, then stay on the N85 to Digne.

Digne-les-Bains (to give it its full title) is one of the best-known stopping places for travellers between Grenoble and the Côte d'Azur, but it is well worth a more leisurely stay. Capital of the Alpes-de-Haute-Provence Department (not to be confused with the Hautes-Alpes Department, of which Gap is the chief town), it stands on the left bank of the Bléone and has many attractions, not only as a health resort with a well-known thermal establishment, but also as both a summer and a winter resort. The original settlement was at the foot of Mount St Vincent, where the village was huddled round the church of Notre-Dame du Bourg, but the present town grew in a more defensible position on the slopes of Mount St Charles. The church is all that now remains of the earlier centre.

The cathedral of St Jerome, heart of the "new" town, was built at the end of the 15th century, partly on the site of the old fortified château which defended the settlement. The medicinal hot springs are a couple of kilometres away to the south along the D20, on the right bank of the Torrent des Eaux Chaudes, which joins the Bleone at Digne. Unusual among French towns, Digne has named its main thoroughfare the Boulevard Gassendi, to commemorate not a politician or a general but a philosopher (1592–1655) who won a Chair of Rhetoric against strong competition when he was only 16, and had many important discussions with Descartes. Digne is well placed for a day trip to the gorges of the Verdon and many other beauty-spots. There are about 15 reasonably priced hotels and pensions and the Syndicat d'Initiative rates three stars.

Gorges of the Verdon

South-eastwards from Digne the N85 goes to Castellane and on through Grasse to the Riviera east of St-Raphael. From Castellane you can turn on to the N555 which leads to Draguignan. Castellane itself is attractively situated on the Verdon river, surrounded by mountains, woodland and open country ranging up to 1980 metres. It has half a dozen accredited hotels and inns and the Syndicat d'Initiative arranges excursions to the nearby places of interest, the best known being the gorges of the Verdon.

The Verdon's Grand Canyon is probably unrivalled in Europe. The Verdon, a tributary of the Durance, has carved a number of dramatic gorges in the limestone plateaux of Haute-Provence, but none of them as deep, precipitous and wild as the Grand Canyon. The north side is best visited by way of the N552 west of Castellane; the south side from Draguignan or Aups. Alternatively the north side can be visited from Moustiers-Ste-Marie, driving east along the N552 towards Castellane.

The south side has the breathtaking Corniche Sublime (D71), a motor road cut through the rock between Comps and Auguine, from which the finest views of the canyon can be seen. The gorges vary in depth from 250 to 700 metres: in width they range (at the bottom) from six to 100 metres, and, at the top of the great cliffs, from 200 to 1500 metres. The north side has other means of approaching the canyon, and it is also possible to explore it on foot (an eight-hour project), but for this you need the right advice, preparation, and clothing.

Draguignan, about 45 km (28 miles) south of Castellane on the N555, is the capital of the Var Department. It is a busy, lively town, best known to holidaymakers today as the gateway to the Verdon gorges and the Maures mountains. It is one of the richest repositories of legend and folk-lore of the south, and there is little doubt that in the same way that Tarascon is named after a particular legendary monster, Draguignan is named after a beast so awe-inspiring as to have been known as *the* Dragon, giving rise to a collection of tales that have become inextricably interwoven with the Christian tradition.

The dragon (Gaelic *drak*) which terrorised the countryside was overcome, according to tradition, by St Hermentaire, first Bishop of Antibes. Unfortunately, as most experts in this field admit, it has been impossible to find any details of the saint's victory, though the victor is said to have built a chapel on the site, dedicated to St Michael. The hermitage of St Hermentaire can be seen when you leave Draguignan in a north-westerly direction.

One authority, quoted by the contemporary French writer Jean-Paul Clébert, suggests that the strength of the tradition, combined with the absence of details, indicates that the Dragon of Draguignan belongs to that class of infernal creatures which inhabit, and are perhaps bred, in marshes, feeding on the devil's plant, the nenuphar, nymphea or, as we call it less ominously, water-lily. Certainly these horrific products of the human imagination suggest the creatures conjured up by miasmic mephitic vapours. The fact remains that the nearby meadows of Nartuby were once part of the marshland that surrounded Draguignan.

From Draguignan it is an easy run to the sea at Ste-Maxime, Frejus or St-Raphael.

The Coast East of Marseilles

Time was when Cassis, the first fishing port-cum-holiday resort east of Marseilles, was precisely that: a fairly busy little port where people from Marseilles and a reasonable number of other French holidaymakers came to relax and drink the delicious white wine which is grown in the hills.

Later came a casino, blocks of flats, more concrete. Today there is a permanent population of about 5000, with a holiday population of something like 20,000 at the peak of the season. Most of the attractive physical features of Cassis are still more or less intact, the old château and remains of the ramparts, the lively port and sharp hills behind the splendidly southern Place Pierre Baragnon (where you will find the two-star Syndicat d'Initiative). The hotels are still led – for old-timers – by the three-star Roches Blanches, and the more modest Hôtel de la Commerce is still there, though the busy Berthe of an earlier day no longer goes from table to table with a huge tureen of soup.

Cap Canaille, the highest cliff in Europe, still rounds off the view superbly, and there are always the *calanques* of Port-Miou, En-Vau and Port Pin, those curious Mediterranean fjords.

La Ciotat, 10 km east of Cassis, has a long and honourable industrial (ship-building) history. It has also the natural dignity of an old sea-coast settlement that bears the magnificently simple name of "The City" (*ciotat–ciudad–civitas*) and is also situated in one of the most beautiful bays of the whole seaboard, sheltered by the cape known as the Bec de l'Aigle, "the eagle's beak". Today La Ciotat has more than 30,000 residents – 60,000 in August. There is provision for most kinds of holidaymaker and no lack of entertainment and interest, including delightful excursions both seawards and inland. Shipyards co-exist happily with the old town and the beach at La Ciotat-Plage. It is a very popular centre for camping, with a wide range of sites. The Syndicat d'Initiative (two-star) is in the Vieux Port.

Between La Ciotat and Bandol is St-Cyr-les-Lecques (or Les Lecques-St-Cyr if you are a citizen of Les Lecques), which consists of the commune of St-Cyr-sur-Mer and the bathing resorts of Les Lecques and La Madrague, which occupy the angles of a triangular plain dominated by wooded hills alongside a two km stretch of fine sand shelving gently to the sea. The normal population of 5000 grows at the peak of the holiday season to 25,000, for whom there is every-thing that sun, sand, sea and the surrounding countryside can offer, including some very pleasant Côtes de Provence wines. La Cadière-Azur, 5 km inland, on a hill with fine views, has a very enjoyable all-purpose red wine, *Cadièrienne*, along with its other attractions, though the new autoroute from Bandol, which cuts a swathe through the valley below Cadière, is a cause of concern to some villagers and visitors.

Bandol, 19 km (12 miles) east of La Ciotat, is the next coastal stop on the N559 from Marseilles. It is a very pleasant, old-established holiday resort that attracted discriminating British visitors long before the mass migrations began. Today it has an impressive array of hotels, headed by the four-star L'Ile Rousse, with another four-star hotel, the Soukana, on the nearby Ile de Bendor. There are five three-star hotels, including two, the Delos and Le Palais, on the Ile de Bendor, and almost a score of other accredited hotels. Bendor is an attractive artistic and sporting centre, only eight minutes off the coast by motor-boat.

Nine kilometres on from Bandol is Sanary, or, to give it its full title, Sanary-sur-Mer-Ollioules, a seaside town whose 10,000 population increases to 40,000 in the season. It is an attractive bathing resort, still with its charming small Mediterranean port nucleus and an 11th century Saracen tower, tucked away in the shelter of the Gulf of St-Nazaire and sheltered from the north by a range of hills. The daily market is no small part of the pleasure of a do-it-yourself

Above: *Pont du Gard, near Nîmes*
Below: *The port, Sainte-Maxime*

La Ciotat

holiday here, and there is no lack of hotels and other accommodation, including camping sites. Historically, Sanary has much to offer besides the Saracen tower; ruins of a feudal château, Roman remains, old houses in the upper village, and fine views from Le Gros Cerveau and Cap Gros. Other excursions can be made to Port Issol, the Red Rocks, Bendor Island and Le Brusc, and inland to the villages of Cadière-Azur, Castellet, and Le Beausset. A motor-racing circuit, a reasonably short distance inland, is also an attraction to some holidaymakers. The Syndicat d'Initiative (two stars) is in the Jardin de la Ville.

Toulon

Toulon has the fascination of all great naval bases, but to the intriguing separateness of the no-entry zones is added a great deal of charm, elegance and, indeed, oddity. The massive re-building operations since the Second World War seem to have lifted some of the heaviness and blankness that tend to haunt the memory of those who knew the city between the wars.

One of the finest harbours in the world, with a normal population of 185,000, rising to 300,000 in the holiday season, it is the southernmost resort of the Côte d'Azur and, within the shelter of the surrounding hills, averages something like 290 days of sunshine a year. With its nearby resorts and countryside, and the wider choice bigger towns always offer in shops, hotels and restaurants, it is a much better bet for the holidaymaker than many of the smaller, much-advertised centres.

Artists and tourists alike are re-discovering the advantages Toulon offers. With the slopes of Mount Faron immediately behind the city and the Gros Cerveau 40 km (25 miles) to the west, Toulon is also within easy reach of St-Mandrier, Le Brusc, Sanary, Bandol, and St-Cyr-les-Lecques. There are regular bus services along the coast ranging from Marseilles on the west to St-Raphael on the east, with further links eastward to Menton and the Italian frontier. In addition, there are special excursions, of which full details can be obtained from the S.I., 3 Boulevard Général Leclerc, 83100, Toulon.

In Toulon itself there is a great deal worth seeing, apart from one of the world's finest roadsteads. There is the Darse Vieille, the Corniche du Mourillon, the great gateway of the arsenal and other magnificent surviving gates, with many fine old and new buildings. There are seven fine collections of art, ethnography and social and architectural history, in addition to the great Naval Museum, and every opportunity for sport, entertainment, music and film-going during the season. Moreover there are sandy beaches, Olympic swimming pools and ample yachting facilities. There is a cable-car service up Mount Faron.

Incidentally, traffic flow, or *circulation* as the French have it (though in most great cities today there is little evidence of either "flow" or "circulation"), is, of course, the main obstacle to using Toulon itself as a holiday base during the peak months. Traffic along the main coast roads becomes a nightmare at times, and although, if one has time, one can always take to the hills to bypass some of the worst bottlenecks, even this is not altogether the answer at certain times of the year, particularly if you are not a totally relaxed, calm and naturally first-class driver with a head for heights and bends.

This is one of the reasons for making the most of Toulon itself, with its inexhaustible interest and animation, the splendid views from its terraced surroundings, and the wealth of history and folk-lore in its naval and military establishments, ancient prison and its inevitable sea legends. One of the latter tells of the Patte-Luzerne (she is also sometimes called the Gallipetun), whose stern had hardly cleared the Toulon roadstead when her bows were already emerging west of the Straits of Gibraltar . . . her decks were covered with cornfields, vineyards and grazing land with abundant cattle, and her masts were so tall that the boys who climbed to the mast-top had white hair and beards by the time they came down on deck again.

Hyères and the Golden Isles

Continuing eastward from Toulon the first port of call on the coast road is Hyères and the Giens Peninsula, with the islands of Porquerolles, Port Cros and the Levant.

Hyères, which normally has 40,000 inhabitants and three times as many in August, has been a celebrated resort since the 18th century: it is at once the oldest and the most southerly holiday resort on the Côte d'Azur. The older parts of the town are terraced on the slopes of the Casteou, the modern districts are mainly in the plain. It has retained a surprising amount of charm in face of the onslaught of urban development and mass holidaymaking, and even during a casual drive through the town, busy as it may be, a feeling of quiet grace, ancient depths and elegance persists. On a tour of the coast from Marseilles to Menton I found that Hyères was one of the places whose flavour had been least affected by undesirable change. Like Menton, it has one of the best climates in the whole of France, and it is still a city to stroll in, either to the fortress on the hill or through the picturesque old streets that radiate from it. The handsome, tree-lined streets of the modern town are no less pleasing to walk in: the modern ant-column of tourists along the Côte seems, without actually doing so, to slow down a little as it passes through Hyères.

The reassuring charm of parts of Hyères itself is a personal and subjective experience. The actual attractions of its surroundings are safer ground for the writer who would like you to enjoy what he has enjoyed. The Fenouillet, for example, offers a pleasant excursion (it can be done comfortably on foot from the old town within two hours, there and back). The Fenouillet (about 300 metres) is the summit of the little Maurettes range which runs from east to west above Hyères. The view from the top is well worth the effort. For the best path and other details call in at the three-star Syndicat d'Initiative in the Place G. Clemenceau.

The principal beaches are at L'Ayguade (four km), Hyères-Plage, a really fine sandy beach (six km), La Capte, on the eastern side of the Giens Peninsula (eight km), and at L'Almanarre (five km) on the road from Hyères to Toulon by way of Carqueiranne. From the town of Hyères to Giens, at the end of the peninsula of that name, there is much of interest. The salt-marshes (Salins des Pesquiers) were formerly étangs (land-locked pools) which were extensively fished: the salt-workings were established in 1850. The lagoon, of which the salt-marshes were once part, separates the two sand stretches of the peninsula. The Madrague road runs along the northern coast of the western tip of the peninsula, with fine views. The village of Giens, which stands on a hill, also offers extensive and beautiful views of coast and sea. At the eastern tip of the peninsula stands La Tour Fondue, a fortress which guards the passage between the mainland and Porquerolles, and is the embarkation point for the Golden Isles. Hyères has one four-star (Le Provençal) five three-star and about 40 other hotels.

The group of islands off the Giens Peninsula, the Iles d'Hyères, or, as they are sometimes called, the Iles d'Or (Golden Isles), consist of Porquerolles (seven km long and about two km wide), Port-Cros (four and a half km long, about two km wide) and the Ile du Levant (eight km long but less than one and a quarter km wide). Porquerolles is one of the most attractive islands off the coast, with rocky coves, tiny creeks, beaches of fine sand and comparative solitude over much of the island. It contains relics of Ligurians, Celts, Etruscans, Greeks (Phocaeans), Romans and Saracens. St Honorat spent some years there before founding his hermitage on the Lerins Islands, off Cannes (AD 375), and it is believed to have been the refuge of the troubadour Rambaud d'Orange, who is said to have celebrated in too precise terms the charms of Queen Marguerite who married Louis IX (St Louis), and of the Man in the Iron Mask while he was in transit between the Château d'If and Ste-Marguerite, in the Lerins.

There are six hotels, four of which are two-star establishments and two more modest. The small port and village of Porquerolles are pleasant. Some years ago a visitor wrote: "In the interior of the island there are few inhabitants, pinewoods, vineyards, and an abundance of African-type vegetation." This flavour of the island is still there, though somewhat modified. Most of the area of Porquerolles was taken under the protection of the State in 1971.

The island of Port-Cros has two three-star hotels and is regarded by its devotees as the most beautiful of the three islands, with a more rugged profile, rising higher from the sea, and with richer greenery, than the others.

The Ile du Levant is best known as one of the favourite spots on the Mediterranean for the naturists, who can enjoy the sun in natural nudity undisturbed.

Porquerolles is accessible from La Tour Fondue (20 min.), Toulon (one and a half hours), from Le Lavandou (one and a half hours), and from Cavalaire by arrangement. Port-Cros is accessible from various points on the Giens Peninsula, from Cavalaire, Le Lavendou and Toulon: Le Levant is accessible from the same embarkation points as Port-Cros. Detailed information about the islands is obtainable from the Syndicat d'Initiative at Hyères. Accommodation in the islands is, in fact, quite limited, so unless you can afford to pay top prices at the last minute make your reservations as early as possible.

Hyères to St-Raphael

From Hyères to St-Raphael is a stretch of coast which includes some of France's best-known resorts, backed by the beautiful hinterland of Les Maures. Some of the resorts have grown so much in the past few decades as to have become almost unrecognisable, others have survived the tourist *putsch* with less obvious damage. But the core of each is still there to be found and the coast between them still has interludes of great and comparatively unspoiled natural beauty.

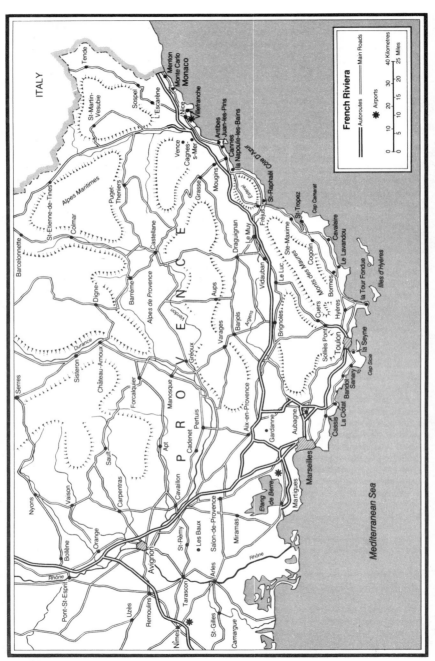

Le Lavandou, which some of us thought we had discovered in the thirties, was a thriving fishing village in the 14th century, and was visited in 1537 by Rabelais on his way to the Ile du Levant. Sheltered by the Pierre d'Avenoun and the Maures *massif*, with one of the finest beaches of the whole coast and other good beaches within easy reach, Le Lavandou, 23 km (14 miles) east of Hyères, was at one time noted for its uncrowded sands and tiny, rather smart village and pricey small shops. Today its basic population is still no more than 3000 or so, but now it has to provide for a July–August influx of something like 50,000.

The built-up area has been formidably extended and the wide range of hotels varies from several four-star establishments to many modest places at the other end of the scale, along with the now almost inevitable motel. Camping sites, of course, account for much of the growing summer population. The hinterland is superb, with the Forest of the Dom, Gassin and Ramatuelle within easy reach, and miles of cork and chestnut woods. The southern vegetable soup, *soupe au pistou*, is particularly good here. The S.I. is on the Quai Baptistin Pins.

A pleasant excursion from Le Lavandou, by way of Bormes-les-Mimosas, through the heavily wooded mountains round Collobrières, includes the village of St-Guillaume (five km from Collobrières on a good road); the Maures Peak of La Sauvette (a four-hour trek there and back on foot); Notre Dame des Anges (four hours there and back on foot, about an hour there and back by car) and, perhaps the most interesting, to the Charterhouse of La Verne.

This superb ruin, situated in one of the loneliest and most beautiful parts of the Maures range, was founded in the 12th century on the northern slope of a ridge between the Verne river and the Mole valley. The buildings were restored in the 18th century but abandoned after the French Revolution. You can reach it by a forest road from the D14 (Collobrières–Grimaud) at a point about six km east of Collobrières. Until recently the last three km had to be completed on foot, now cars can drive right up to the monastery. The magnificent remaining masses of ancient stonework, spread out over their mountain eyrie, have a splendid main entrance in serpentine stone with a beautiful small cloister of the same materials. The views from the site are breathtaking, and in the season the custodians of the building provide simple refreshments of bread, cheese and wine. A pleasant way back to Bormes is by the Col de Babaou, along which it is worth keeping a weather eye open on your left for an extraordinary Victorian–Gothic private chapel in the middle of the chestnut and cork woods: it stands out like a construction by the American artist Joseph Cornell.

Cavalière, which is part of the commune of Le Lavandou, also has a fine, sandy beach in a setting of pinewoods, and although it must in the season take much of Le Lavandou's overspill, it gives the impression of being one of the less aggressively developed resorts. It has a few excellent hotels, details of which are obtainable from the Syndicat d'Initiative at Le Lavandou.

Continuing eastwards, after Cavalière comes Le Rayol-Le Canadel-sur-mer, a cumbrous title for the coast at Canadel and the pleasant holiday resort of Le Rayol which faces the Isles of Hyères. Le Canadel and Le Rayol between them have about ten hotels (including the four-star Bailli de Suffren, which is on the sea at Le Rayol), good beaches, masses of flowers, and wooded *calanques*, or fjords, backed by the Pradels hills. Henry Royce, partner of C. S. Rolls and designer of many of the well-known cars that bore their joint names, once lived here.

From Le Rayol to Cavalaire, the next resort, is still a beautiful coast drive. Cavalaire itself, though its population figures are comparable with those of Le Lavandou, amounting to just under 3000 normally, and about 40,000 in August, gives a much more discouraging impression of sheer size. This may be because it has two and a half miles of beach and the enormous amount of building that has gone on sprawls all over the place to make the most of the sea-front. It certainly struck me as the most drastically developed of the smaller places.

But whatever Cavalaire has suffered aesthetically, many more thousands of people have had splendid holidays here than could have done years ago. With at least a score of hotels, many of them very good indeed, every facility the average holidaymaker needs, and such lovely old Provençal villages as Gassin, Ramatuelle and Grimaud within easy reach, it is not surprising that it now has a two-star Syndicat d'Initiative (Square de Lattre-de-Tassigny) to help the ever-increasing tide of visitors.

From Cavalaire to St-Tropez the way lies through La Croix-Valmer, in the vine-covered hills that shelter the bay of Cavalaire to the north, and then by the winding Col de Collebasse, with fine views. Before taking the main N98 into St-Tropez it would be well worth while having a look at the hill village of Gassin, the Mills of Paillas, and, if you can so arrange your journey, the village of Grimaud. But these can also be conveniently visited from St-Tropez if you decide to move in there first and stay for a while.

St-Tropez

St-Tropez is a place of extraordinary contradictions. Sometimes described as a summer resort which has fairly recently become fashionable, its "in" period was quite some time ago and it is regarded nowadays as trendy only in mass-circulation newspapers which are invariably many fashions out of date. It is also about the only resort on the Côte d'Azur which turns its back firmly on the Mediterranean and faces north. Its reputation as the favourite spot of "the beautiful people" has resulted in its having more spectators than spectacle, and it is hardly possible to see its originally beautiful waterfront for the bulbous and top-heavy "luxury" yachts which have replaced the old fishing boats.

None the less, the features that first attracted celebrated holiday-makers are still there, if you dig for them. Much of the old town is charming, there are quiet corners away from the blatantly commercial quays and the views inland towards the Maures and seaward over the old town from the Mole du Portalet are still fascinating. Its basic population of nearly 7000 is estimated to grow to 64,000 in the season – that is in July and August – but even during a week-end in June it can be as crowded as Brighton on a Bank Holiday. You may occasionally see a famous face, but most of them have found less exposed corners away from the port.

After the initial shock of the overcrowded port there are some delightful surprises round the corner, where you can eat in peace and even look out over a quiet few yards of beach with a working-boat lying by the wall. But these you must seek out for yourselves: it is well worth it. There is a superb serpentine doorway to the 18th century church in the old town and the chapel of St Anne, with its views over St-Tropez and the gulf, is worth a visit (about one km along the D93 southwards towards Pampelonne, plus a seven minute climb on foot). The beaches, of course, are splendid – not only Pampelonne but also the other beaches, the Graniers, Tahiti, the Salins, the Bouillabaisse and others. There are festivals of all kinds, including two *bravades*, one on May 16, 17 and 18, the other – *Bravade des Espagnols* – on June 15. These are associated more or less historically with the musketeers who tried to repel the pirates who attacked the town incessantly in the 15th century. The old Citadel, on its knoll to the east of the town, is the setting for the *Nuits de la Citadelle* in July and August. And above all, St-Tropez is within easy reach of many of the most beautiful of those inland attractions which can make you smile quietly to yourself when you hear people who know only the overcrowded parts of the coast disparaging the Côte d'Azur. These include Ramatuelle, Cogolin, Cap Camarat, and the Chartreuse de la Verne.

On the other side of the Gulf of St-Tropez is Ste-Maxime, which faces due south and attracts something like 35,000 visitors in the high summer. It has fine sand, first-class hotels and St-Tropez across the gulf, either as an added attraction or as a place you would rather look at than stay in. The two-star S.I. is in the Boulevard de la Republique.

Tucked away in the gulf is Port Grimaud, the creation of one man, François Spoerry. This lagoon village is similar in conception to the new resorts of Languedoc-Roussillon, in that it was built on a stretch of salt-marsh and sand-dunes. The houses are curiously pleasing and effective imitations of traditional Mediterranean, and the village has everything the yachtsman could want, including a number of good, expensive restaurants. An English writer who has made a special study of the French Mediterranean harbours has called it "a three-dimensional *trompe l'oeil* in good taste". It is also expensive.

The next stage of the journey east towards St-Raphael, where, according to today's conventions, the Riviera itself begins (and joins its Italian counterpart at Ventimiglia), is reached at St-Aygulf, which is linked with Fréjus. The setting of St-Aygulf is as attractive as only this coast can ensure, sheltered as it is with pinewoods and groves of oak and cork-oak. There is a beach of fine sand, surrounded by rocks. The extent to which it has grown over recent years can be measured by the fact that its permanent population of 3000 or so goes up to nearly 40,000 in July and August. Much of this is accounted for by campers and caravanners, as it offers some of the best sites along the coast. There is also an adequate range of hotels and a Syndicat d'Initiative to cope with all inquiries. For sun, sea and sand, St-Aygulf fills the bill: for other entertainment, night-life and cultural interests Fréjus supplies the need, with Roman remains, cinemas, even *corridas*. Fréjus itself, which lies between the Maures range and the Esterel, and leads on to St-Raphael, is best considered, however, as the introduction to the next chapter, the Riviera itself.

Antibes sea-wall

Côte d'Azur –
St-Raphael to
Monaco and Menton

If you are concerned with saving time and effort, one way to reach the Riviera is to step into an aeroplane at London airport on a dull, cool, cloudy, unappetising London night, and step out less than two hours later into the warm, flower-scented, star-filled, sea-sparkling night at Nice airport.

But to go south by road offers abundant rewards and, if you have time to digress, rich discoveries.

The most familiar road route to the Riviera itself is down the Rhône valley by the A7 autoroute (formerly by the N7), and then by way of Aix-en-Provence across the magnificent country behind Toulon, to join the coast at Fréjus-St-Raphael, then on through Cannes, Nice and so on. There is also an excellent mountain route which is not too rigorous, over the Col de la Croix-Haute to Sisteron and Digne, with the alternative through Gap to Digne, and St-André-des-Alpes and Entrevaux.

Thirdly, you can, if you are a first-class mountain driver, take the summer route south along the N202 over the *Izoard pass* (2360 metres) to Guillestrè, and then over the Vars pass (2011 metres) to Barcelonnette. From Grenoble to Barcelonnette by the two passes is 135 km (84 miles).

Barcelonnette to St-Raphael

Barcelonnette, which stands at 1135 metres and has 3400 inhabitants, is perfectly situated as a summer and winter resort (it is practically surrounded by winter-sports centres). From Barcelonnette towards the coast every route has its scenic attractions. The N208, for example, leads over the Allos pass (2250 metres) through Allos and Colmar. About nine km south of Colmar the road divides, N208 continuing to Annot, N55 bearing right to St-André-les-Alpes. I would recommend taking the right fork, even if it lengthens your journey a little, for the pleasure of seeing St-André-les-Alpes, a good example of the kind of mountain village – or very small town – that brings many holidaymakers back to the south year after year, and compensates in good measure for some of the more regrettable developments along the coast itself.

St-André, with its Syndicat d'Initiative in the Rue Basse, does in fact see its modest population of just over 1000 doubled in July and August, but much of the increase is absorbed by the excellent camping sites in the surrounding countryside, and the village in the high season is characterised by greater animation rather than congestion. It has eight hotels, four in the starred categories, and the S.I. has a list of available lettings for the summer. St-André loses nothing by being a little overlooked in the general publicity for this area: the visitor does not expect anything sensational and is agreeably surprised: you could do worse than take a very relaxed spell in St-André and its mountain setting.

From St-André the N207 comes down the mountains by way of Entrevaux and Puget-Theniers to Nice, or by the N85 through Castellane and Grasse to Cannes. One of the advantages of the first route is that it takes you through Entrevaux, a lovely and still-unspoiled mountain township with an ancient cathedral, a fortress, defence works by Vauban and a particularly fine situation. Local accommodation is limited – there are only three hotels and one camping site – but the popular township of Annot, also based on an old fortified village on the N208 about 10 km away, has six or seven hotels and is more adequately, though not excessively, geared to holidaymakers.

Annot can also be reached directly from Barcelonnette by keeping to the N208, but this would mean bypassing St-André-les-Alpes, which I think would be a pity.

The route through St-André-les-Alpes also provides for the alternative way to the coast, through Grasse. From St-André drive south along the N207 (which goes to Entrevaux and eventually Nice) until you come to a secondary road turning off to the right (N555). This takes you to Castellane, on the N85. Castellane is a health resort on the Verdon river, surrounded by mountains, woodland and fields ranging up to 1980 metres. Castellane itself, which stands at 724 metres, has considerable charm with a Romanesque church, pentagonal tower, Clock Gate, old ramparts and Napoleon bridge, as well as the Chapel of Notre-Dame du Roc, outside the township, from which there are fine views.

It is probably the most practical base for a visit to the Grand Canyon of the Verdon, which makes an unforgettable whole-day trip from Castellane. The town itself is attractive with its fine central square, the Place Marcel Sauvaire, and has nine comparatively small family hotels, details of which can be obtained from the Syndicat d'Initiative, Castellane. There is a superabundance of mainly high-grade camping and caravan sites in the neighbourhood.

From Castellane the N85 (Route Napoleon) runs directly to Grasse and Cannes.

The last important town on the main Rhône valley route to the Riviera before it reaches the coast, Fréjus almost adjoins St-Raphael, with which it is associated in most holidaymakers' minds. The city took its name from Forum Julii, a village founded by Julius Caesar in 49 BC, and is sometimes called the "Pompeii of Provence" because of its Roman remains. It is certainly a worthy gateway to the most famous stretch of the whole of the French Mediterranean coast.

Fréjus – or, to give it its full name, Fréjus-Ville et Fréjus-Plage – is a town of 30,000 which grows to 100,000 in the season. Apart from its wide range of Roman remains, it has a 13th century cathedral, a 12th century cloister and a 5th century baptistery. With every kind of entertainment and sport for holidaymakers (including *corridas*), it is well situated where the range of mountains known as Les Maures gives way to the beautiful stretch known as the Esterel, and offers, among its many local attractions, excursions to Mont Vinaigre and the Pic de l'Ours (through the forest of the Esterel).

Fréjus-Ville and Fréjus-Plage share between them about two dozen hotels, with the four-star Grand and the three-star Oasis on the beach. There is a Syndicat d'Initiative in each section. Camping and caravan sites are legion in the neighbourhood, and there are other kinds of accommodation, such as youth hostels and holiday houses for families.

St-Raphael, "gateway to the Esterel", once a smallish, elegant winter and summer resort, has grown during the past 20 years almost out of all recognition, a process which has been aggravated by the fact that it is the point at which the bulk of the Riviera-bound traffic hits the coast, creating, at times, bottlenecks of world championship calibre. It is ironical to recall that Alphonse Karr, the French journalist who put St-Raphael on the map in the 1860s, took a house there because he had found this little corner of the coast quieter than Nice. It was not long before he was trying to persuade his friends – writers, painters and musicians – to join him at St-Raphael. Earlier, in the 18th century, St-Raphael became temporarily famous as the landing place of Napoleon Bonaparte's ships on their victorious return from Egypt. In 1814, Napoleon visited St-Raphael again, only this time in defeat and on his way to exile in Elba.

The town's normal population of fewer than 20,000 goes up to 100,000 in August, and its three-star Syndicat d'Initiative in the Square Gallieni is kept busy supplying information, advice and guidance. Here, and in the neighbouring Boulouris, accommodation is on the scale of a major resort. There are more than 60 hotels (from four-star downwards) in and around St-Raphael, and the S.I. can provide a formidable list of letting agencies. There are many camping and caravan sites.

St-Raphael to Cannes

The next resort, going east along the coast road, N98 (the Corniche d'Or, or Corniche of the Esterel, which runs from St-Raphael to La Napoule and then rejoins the N7), is Agay, in a stretch of red cliffs, overlooked by the ridge of the Rastel (over 300 metres). This is the heart of the red cliffs, classical pines and azure sea section of the coast. Along this stretch every resort has a beautiful setting, marred only by indiscriminate development here and there along the coast roads and the apparently inevitable pollution problems of a tideless sea liable to be contaminated by both human waste and oil.

Even more dramatically pictorial is the next resort, Anthéor, where the red rocky cliffs are deeply indented by the sea. Anthéor-Plage, which is part of the Commune of St-Raphael, is set against the backcloth of Cap Roux and the wooded hills of the Esterel. Accommodation at Anthéor-Plage itself is comparatively limited, but there is a camping-caravan site. Le Trayas, nine km farther east, which has a beach of sand and shingle, is in terraces at the foot of the Esterel, and has a particularly attractive beach, surrounded by rocks, at La Figueirette and Notre Dame.

From Le Trayas the road goes round the Pointe de l'Esquillon (Esquillon headland), by way of Miramar, a resort on the southern slope of the headland, to Théoule. Théoule is a thriving holiday centre which has grown rapidly from a tiny, semi-circular beach with two or three shops, one small hotel (l'Auberge de la Corniche d'Or, which serves excellent fish soup), and one expensive hotel with its own tiny bay, to become a very popular resort with several good hotels (one four-star), excellent beaches, and a starred Syndicat d'Initiative. A little farther on is La Napoule-Plage, or, to give it its official name, Mandelieu-Napoule. This resort has over a dozen starred hotels, sandy beaches on the sea and on the River Siagne, art exhibitions, every kind of water-sport and recreation, including Mandelieu race-course, and Cannes within easy reach (eight km). The setting of La Napoule is attractive, lying as it does at the foot of the rock of San Peyre (about 140 metres), and the village has a restored château with 14th century towers. This was restored in 1919 by Henry Clews, an American sculptor, and now contains the La Napoule Henry Clews Memorial Art Foundation, with works by the donor.

Cannes

The first time I visited Cannes a guide-book of that period said that it owed its success to the beauty of its situation, the mildness of its climate and the magnificence of the festivals held there. It also described the town, quoting an unnamed source, as "the winter salon of the world's aristocracy", which was also acquiring popularity as a summer resort.

That was quite a few years ago. Today its year-round population is over 68,000, swollen to 100,000 in July and August. It has an International Film Festival, a Festival of Amateur Films, a Festival of Advertising Films and many other festivals related mainly to the business side of pop music, television and other commercial arts. It has an international fireworks festival and has even retained some of its own local customs, including the comparatively recent "battle of flowers", and regattas, and (not to be missed) some intensely local and deep-rooted celebrations which take place on and around the dramatic hill, Mont Chevalier or the Colline du Suquet, which dominates the old port and what remains of the old town. Among the best-known, one of the most beautiful is the Mimosa Festival in February. Curiously enough mimosa was first imported to Cannes as comparatively recently as 1835: today about 1500 acres are devoted to its cultivation, mainly for export.

Cannes has, naturally, one of the best-equipped Syndicats d'Initiative (four stars) in the Palais des Festivals et des Congrès, La Croisette. It has also, in addition to high-speed links with Nice airport, regular shipping-line services to New York, Central and Southern America, and the main Mediterranean ports. Of its well over 100 hotels, eight are in the top-level, four-star-plus, category and no fewer than eight in the four-star bracket.

Cannes acquired its English popularity when, in 1834, Lord Brougham, then England's Chancellor, was on his way to Nice and discovered that a cholera epidemic in Provence had "closed the frontier" at the Var. Lord Brougham turned back and decided to spend his holiday in Cannes, then little more than a small fishing port. He liked it so much that he returned there every winter for 34 years, and was gradually joined by most of the English aristocracy, including the Princes of Wales, later Edward VII, who became a regular visitor.

Those who still like to imagine what the old Cannes was like are drawn to the Mont Chevalier, with its 17th century church of Notre-Dame de l'Espèrance and the square tower and other relics of the ancient château of the Abbots of Lerins: below is the old town and port; from the hill the views are superb, particularly on festival nights.

Of course, the amount of building and development has changed the character of Cannes as a whole, but there are still quiet corners and there is more than enough in the way of music and entertainment all the year round for the growing numbers of middle-aged and elderly French people who are making it their permanent home. There is no lack of highly organised beaches: Palm Beach has its world-famous Casino; the promenade and beaches of the Croisette extend for almost two km from the gardens of the Municipal Casino to Palm Beach Casino and the Cap de la Croisette. If you find the beaches crowded, and the spectacle less elegant than you had imagined, content yourself with enjoying the magnificent seaward view and the cluster of the old town: as someone once wrote, it is perhaps better to live opposite a beautiful view than in it. The harbours are now so well geared to the pleasure-yacht business that the sybarite hardly needs to leave his floating home except for an evening on the town, and as for coping with the short-based waves and sudden bad-tempered outbursts of the off-shore Mediterranean, he can leave that to the hardier spirits.

But whatever Cannes may have lost of its old charm and earlier elegance, it still has its share of the hinterland, which has not yet been irretrievably spoilt.

There are enjoyable trips to be made to Super-Cannes and the Observatory of La Californie above the town; to Le Pézou, from which the view over the Gulf of La Napoule, the Esterel, Grasse and the foothills of the Alps is magnificent; and, from the old town in the west, to the Croix des Gardes, at the top of a 164-metre hill. Farther out there is Vallauris, with its potteries, and Golfe Juan; Antibes and the Plateau de la Garoupe on the Cape; the Massif de l'Esterel, Mandelieu, and Mougins. And among the most attractive sea-trips is one to the off-shore Lerins Islands. St-Honorat and Ste-Marguerite. But do not be surprised if the not-always-docile Mediterranean gives you a sharp shake-up on the way to the islands in a smallish boat – it will make the pleasure of sailing into the lovely calm plateau between the islands all the more enjoyable.

Ste-Marguerite

Ste-Marguerite, the larger and higher of the two islands, is not much more than one km off-shore. It is a pleasant, wooded spot, with a fortified château from the terrace of which there are fine views. St-Honorat, separated from Ste-Marguerite by the narrow, placid channel known as the Plateau du Milieu, looks more forbidding than the other island but is also beautifully wooded and well worth a visit. The ancient fortified monastery, on a point of the island, is visible from a considerable distance.

The islands are exceptionally rich, even for this area, in folk-lore, both religious and pagan. One of the most charming tales is that Ste Marguerite (according to local legend the sister of St Honorat) was so fond of her brother that she could not bear the separation enforced by the fact that men were not allowed to set foot on Ste-Marguerite, and women were banned from St-Honorat. St Honorat, touched by this devotion, nevertheless remained firm except for one concession: he would see his sister once a year, when the cherry-trees were in bloom. Ste Marguerite prayed so long and so devoutly for an extension of this privilege that eventually one cherry-tree in the island was allowed to blossom every month.

Ste-Marguerite island is also associated with the Man in the Iron Mask, the 17th century's unknown political prisoner, who was incarcerated in the Fort Ste-Marguerite in 1687 and transferred to the Bastille in 1698. East of the Ile St-Honorat the tiny Ilot de St-Ferreol contained for a time the tomb of Paganini, who died of cholera in Nice in 1840. In 1845 his remains were transferred to Genoa.

Grasse to Nice

Grasse, 18 km (11 miles) north of Cannes at the junction of the N85 with N562 and N567, stands on the southern slopes of Roquevignon, which shelters it from the north. At an altitude ranging between 206 and 526 metres, with a population of over 12,000, it has a three-star Syndicat d'Initiative at 6, Place de la Foux. The old town is delightful, with its basically 12th century cathedral and watch-tower, its Fragonard Museum, which also houses a regional collection, and the Hôpital du Petit-Paris, the chapel of which possesses three paintings by Rubens.

In the Middle Ages, Grasse was a republic administered by a council of "consuls" on the Italian model, and it remained in close relationship with Pisa until the Comte de Provençe, Raymond-Berenger, terminated this arrangement, as well as Grasse's independent existence, in 1227. The French painter, Jean-Honoré Fragonard (1732–1806) was born in Grasse, son of a tanner-glovemaker who had hoped that his son, failing to become a competent craftsman, might become a clerk. The son is honoured in Grasse today as a great painter.

Fragonard's father, incidentally, was a true representative of the older Grasse, in which tanning, soap-making and weaving were the major industries. Scent-making began in the 16th century when a Florentine settled in Grasse, and saw the possibilities of exploiting the rosemary and lavender from the mountains. By the 18th century the master perfumers were already a powerful group. In the 19th century flower-cultivation and scent-making entirely supplanted the older occupations. Apart from Fragonard, Grasse's most famous son was François de Grasse, Admiral of France (1723–88) who opposed the English during the American War of Independence. Visitors who made Grasse fashionable as a health resort included Pauline Borghese (Napoleon I's sister) and, later, Queen Victoria, who spent several winters there and established a pattern for the British.

The surroundings of Grasse are particularly pleasant, including as they do the gorges of the Loup and a wealth of excursions to such mountain villages as Gréolières, Gourdon and Cabris, and other places of interest such as the Grotto of St Cezaire, and, only 37 km (23 miles) north of Grasse, the winter-sports resort of Thorenc. Immediately northwards from Thorenc lies the lovely mountain region of St-André-les-Alpes, Castellane, Annot and Entrevaux.

Immediately east of Cannes is Golfe-Juan, Juan-les-Pins, Cap d'Antibes, Antibes, Cros-de-Cagnes, St-Laurent-du-Var and Nice, to name only the principal points. This is the region where the Loup and the Var reach the sea and here again the hinterland makes up for some of the things that have happened to the coast. Behind the rather featureless seaside town which is the beachhead of Cagnes lies what is now called Cagnes-sur-Mer, a description which includes the hill village, Haut-de-Cagnes. The physical structure of the village and the views it offers are still beautiful despite some commercialisation. And beyond Cagnes is a partly domesticated but still-ravishing countryside of woodland and peaks, lush valleys and rocky outcrops with villages perched on them like Noah's Ark on Ararat.

Antibes

Antibes is, like Menton, among the élite of the older attractions of the South of France in that these, and few other places, have best survived the onslaught of mass tourism.

What has to some extent saved Antibes is its position tucked away on the eastern side of the rocky peninsula which is Cap d'Antibes. This means that, like other favoured capes along the Mediterranean coast, the main motor roads that scar the coast from end to end shoot across the neck of the peninsula, so that you have the two-fold advantage of ease of access and a comforting detachment from the main stream of traffic.

Antibes, or Antibes–Juan-les-Pins, Alpes-Maritimes, to give the joint communes their full title, have a permanent population of something like 40,000 inhabitants, but in the summer season visitors swell this number enormously, particularly in Juan. But although they now form one municipality, not only Antibes and Juan, but also Cap d'Antibes itself, fully justify separate consideration.

Antibes belongs not only to "tourism" but to history. Founded during the 5th century BC by the Greeks (Phocoeans) who were already established in Massilia (Marseilles), on the site of a Ligurian camp as part of a chain of trading posts, it was called Antipolis, and history-proud local people still like to call themselves *Antipolitains* as an alternative to *Antibois*. The Greek colonists had their problems with the Ligurian tribes, and the Romans stepped in during the 2nd century AD, eventually taking over the whole area. Antibes, like Marseilles, held out for a long time before becoming a Roman city, but in the end a Roman fortified settlement rose on the site of the Greek acropolis, where the Château Grimaldi, with the museum incorporating a unique Picasso collection, now stands.

Successive invasions and battles wrought havoc in the old city, and in the 19th century a new town was built to the west of the old one, with its centre in what is now the Place de Gaulle. But enough remains of the old town to make it one of the most fascinating places of the whole coast. The ramparts have been largely retained, with houses built into them, and the one-way motor road which winds between the ramparts and the sea is one of old Antibes's main attractions. Narrow alleys and stairways under arches lead from the seaward road through the precincts of the château and the cathedral to the market and the ancient streets that plunge down through what remains of the old town towards the new. It is a complex of endless interest.

Between Nice and Cannes, and sheltered to the west by the Cape, Antibes makes the best of both worlds – the old and the new. There is still a pleasant combination of a normal, busy, day-to-day life in an ancient centre of civilisation and the thriving activity of a contemporary small port. The *Antibois* of the new town and the *Antipolitains* of the old are equally proud of the Picasso collection in the château and the care with which the houses clustered within the ramparts have been restored and preserved. And there is, among the Graeco-Roman remains of Antipolis preserved in the archaeological section of the museum, what must be one of the ancient world's most touching relics – a tablet in memory of the boy Septentrion, a 12-year-old who came to the city with a company of actors and dancers before the end of the 2nd century AD, danced for two days to the delight of his audience, and died. Neither the exact date nor the cause of death is stated – but seven palm-leaves in bas-relief symbolise the seven stars by which navigators find the North Star, and also symbolise the dancer's name: Septentrion.

Antibes, Cap d'Antibes and Juan-les-Pins have some of the best hotels of the whole coast. One has only to think of the Baie Dorée-Maison du Gouverneur and the Mapotel Tananarive – both four-star establishments – plus a score of other hotels, in Antibes itself; over a dozen hotels, headed by the Hotel du Cap-Eden Roc and La Résidence du Cap, on Cap d'Antibes, and almost 70 hotels in Juan les Pins, headed by five four-star establishments, Belles-Rives, Helios, Juana, Beau-Séjour, and Parc – of which the first three are rated as four-star plus – to realise how the supply of first-class accommodation has grown in recent years.

From Antibes to Nice there are about 20 km (12 miles) of one of the dreariest coast roads in France, unredeemed even by the dramatic, if inappropriate, concrete ziggurats or pyramids which have sprung up in recent years on the edge of the sea. It is a fast road on which the driver is the most fortunate occupant of any car, in that he is obliged to keep his attention on the rest of the traffic until it is time to turn off for Nice airport or inland to find an oasis in the concrete. It combines the worst kind of ribbon development with long stretches of nothingness between the road and the sea – beaches which appear to be without a local habitation or a name, wastelands not of nature but of man. These empty quarters are relieved – if that is the word – here and there by karting tracks and other diversions which look as though they have been dumped haphazardly between the road and the beach. For the rest there are motels, garish shopping centres, playgrounds, Chinese junks, every kind of mechanical amusement it is possible for man in his desperation to devise. It must be one of the world's most appalling monuments to the failure of imagination, environmental responsibility, intelligent planning and control, preferable only to the much more harmful pollution of the seas. For if this stretch of road has been reduced to a meaningless track between two points, there is the sea on one side and a still-marvellous hinterland on the other, and if the fun-places give pleasure to some of the holidaymakers all is not lost, and it may be easier one day to repair the harm done here than ever it will be to cleanse the worst stretches of the coast.

From Antibes, however, there are pleasant trips west and then north, by the D35 and the N85 to Mougins and Grasse. And due north from Antibes, along the by-ways from the coast road, it is a comparatively short run to Biot (N7 and D4, eight km). Biot, which has become something of a shrine for admirers of the work of Fernand Léger, the French painter and ceramics artist, still retains much of its village quality, perched on a low hill with fewer than 3000 inhabitants. It has a charming arcaded *place* with a 15th-century church, and is an important centre for the production of grapes for the table, as well as flowers for the perfume industry at Grasse.

About 10 km along the coast road from Antibes to Nice, a left turn into the N85 can be the beginning of many other pleasant excursions. If you keep to the N85 you come almost immediately to Villeneuve-Loubet, a pleasant hill-town of nearly 4000 people, with a Syndicat d'Initiative at the Mairie, an hotel and five well-recommended motels and the Musée Auguste Escoffier, a museum of the culinary art. It is only about two km from Cagnes and three km from the coast, and contains a house which was the property of Marshal Pétain and is now a children's home.

Alternatively, soon after turning into the N85, the D36 forks left to Cagnes, St-Paul-de-Vence, Vence and, by various delectable digressions, to Tourette-sur-Loup, Coursegoules, St-Jeannet and many other pleasant spots. Another attractive route to Tourette-sur-Loup and to a whole chain of mountain villages begins at Villeneuve-Loubet, where the D7A, a right-turn off the N85, leads into the N7 and opens up a fascinating area to explore.

Cagnes, which we have already briefly noticed, is still a typical Provençal hill village, with old houses built into its ramparts. Between them, Haut-de-Cagnes (the hill village) and Cros-de-Cagnes (the little port with a beach) have over 22,000 inhabitants and a two-star Syndicat d'Initiative. The old village has a Renoir museum in the painter's former house, and many art galleries and exhibitions. There are about 15 hotels, mostly in Le Cros, and many camping and caravan sites in the area. St-Paul-de-Vence is a particularly attractive old hill village, with the additional distinction that it also has the Fondation Maeght, which is claimed to be the most modern art gallery and art centre in

Gourdon

Above: *The beaches of La Croisette, Cannes*
Below: *The old town, Nice*

Europe. Beautifully situated on the hill known as the Colline de St-Paul, with terraced gardens, superb views, and sculpture effectively placed in the grounds, it consists of a number of well-designed buildings planned and designed by the architect Jose Luis Sert and decorated by some of the greatest artists of our time. It is intended to be an artistic and cultural meeting place as well as an art gallery, and concerts and ballets are held there.

St-Paul has a picturesque Provençal fountain, medieval ramparts, a charming Provençal museum consisting of a replica of a 19th century peasant's house, and an interesting collection of modern paintings in the Colombe d'Or. The S.I. is in the Maison de la Tour, Rue Grande.

Vence

Near St-Paul is Vence itself, a delightful hill town sheltered from the north winds by the great limestone walls of the Baous (the Provençal name for rocky peaks), such as the Baou des Blancs (673 metres), the Baou St-Jeannet (over 400 metres) and the Puy de Tourettes (well over 1000 metres). The promontory on which the town stands is more than 350 metres high and the light has an almost Greek quality. The purity of its famous spring of La Foux is known throughout the south, and the views from its old streets and archways would in themselves make a visit worth while. With just over 9000 inhabitants and a two-star S.I. in the Place du Grand Jardin, it offers a great deal to holiday-makers and to its fortunate permanent residents.

The 11th century cathedral has Roman fragments built into the walls. There are five gates to the city, of which the most interesting is the Peyra Gate, through which one walks to the Place Peyra with its lovely Peyra Fountain and 15th century tower. Outside the city there are many pleasant walks and drives (the S.I. produces a special handbook to these), among which a visit to the Chapelle du Rosaire, on the St-Jeannet road (called Avenue Henri-Matisse) should not be missed.

This is the chapel designed and decorated for the Dominican Sisters of Monteils (Aveyron) by the French painter Matisse, who died in Nice in 1954, aged 84. Walls, floor and ceiling are of white marble, the altar is of the warm-coloured stone from Rogny which the Romans used to build the Pont du Gard. The stained-glass windows are in luminous tints of lime yellow, the green of fresh young shoots, and a pure Mediterranean blue. Matisse's line-drawings on white tiles echo the black-and-white of Dominican garments, but in daylight they are bathed in a brilliant, almost unearthly radiance from the windows. The artist himself said that what he had attempted to do was to take a confined space and, by the interplay of colour and line, create the impression of infinity. The chapel is open to the public on Tuesdays and Thursdays unless religious festivals fall on those days. Work began on the chapel in 1947, when Matisse was 77, and the completed building was consecrated on June 25, 1951, three years before the artist's death.

A pleasant 17 km (10 miles) run from Vence by the D2 takes you over the Col de Vence to Coursegoules, a tiny village of sheep-farmers at about 1000 metres, with the backcloth of the Cheiron (about 1900 metres).

East and north-east of Vence, in the upper reaches of the Cagnes, there are many attractive routes and places. St-Jeannet, at the foot of the Baou de St-Jeannet, is quiet and restful, with magnificent views. Although table grapes have largely taken the place of wine production, there is still available, if you ask in the right places, a white wine of St-Jeannet with something of the radiance and clarity of the Matisse chapel.

Below St-Jeannet, in the Vallon de la Cagne, where the stripling river tumbles fresh and sparkling over rocks and rapids in friendly ravines, there are a number of ancient mills. If country quiet in the mountains, with a stream at your door and fireflies to light your evening stroll, appeals to you, seek out this corner of France. A tough little car is desirable but not entirely indispensable. There are tracks where a mule would be more useful. If you stay long enough you will find that you can, in fact, walk everywhere you want to go: beyond that there are buses from Vence or St-Jeannet.

Within easy reach are the pleasant Tourette-sur-Loup to the west, La Gaude, Gattières, Carros and many other excellent *points-de-repère* to the north, with the winter resorts of Valberg and Auron still farther north. If you propose to explore the Vence area in detail I recommend the French Carte de France, 1/50,000, Type 1922, Feuilles XXXVI 42–43–44 and adjoining sections.

One of the impressive, if not exactly picturesque, views you get from La Gaude is the industrial zone of Nice along the bank of the Var below you. It appears to be an imaginative development which attracts workers from many of the villages where scenic beauty and the tourist trade are not really enough to stimulate and feed the out-going younger generation. Local workers have the choice of living in the industrial zone or commuting from their hill villages, which will thus, it is hoped, not be entirely abandoned to the old and the holidaymakers.

Nice

The Var, once described as "before 1860 a line of demarcation between the easy-going semi-Italian people to the east and the more energetic French population to the west . . .", brings us to Nice, capital of the Côte d'Azur and, with a population of 350,000, one of France's great cities.

The differences in character between Nice and Cannes are too complex to be gone into here, but almost everybody who knows this coast well has a marked preference for one or the other. Rarely do you find the anti-crowds, anti-big-city visitor who dislikes them both. Most often, in my experience, the visitor, offered a theoretical choice of spending some time in either city, will say, "After all, there is something rather special about Nice . . ."

Nice is not only the four-star-plus Negresco and almost 300 other officially listed hotels, it is also the *Babazouk* – the old town and port. It is not only elaborate carnivals and flower festivals, but also a university city of growing academic and general cultural importance. It is not only the spacious Place Masséna, but also the Cours Saleya and the flower market. As befits its size and interest it has a four-star S.I. in the Bureau National de la Chaine d'Acceuil at 13, Place Masséna, with a social and valuable service called Accueil de France. This enables the visitor to book rooms for the same day or the following day in hotels in Nice and in all other resorts served by the Bureau

National de la Chaine National d'Accueil et Information – a service for which no booking charge is made.

Historically, Nice, founded in 350 BC by the Greeks of Marseilles as a small trading post, is of great interest. The site of the original settlement was on the Rocher du Château (Castle Rock) and on the left bank of the mouth of the Paillon, the river which forms the dividing line between the old and new towns today, and has been partly covered in and built over. Prehistoric remains have been found in the caves of the rock. There seems no doubt that there was a Ligurian camp on the hill of Cimiez, but the city really began in the Greek market settlement on the rock, which was given the proud name of Nike (Victory). The Romans later preferred the Cimiez site, but both centres were destroyed in the barbarian invasions. An unimportant little township, which was all that was left of Nice, then passed from the power of one lordling to another until 1388, when it came under the Duke of Savoy's protection.

In the 17th and 18th centuries Nice was bandied back and forth between France and Italy until the unification of Italy followed an alliance between Napoleon III and Victor-Emmanuel of Savoy Piedmont in 1859, when Nice and Savoy were returned to France. Older members of the present generation will remember Mussolini's abortive battle-cry – "*Nice, Tunis, Corsica!*"

Nice is a marvellous city of museums and galleries. Furniture, paintings and Provençal pottery are in the Musée Masséna, a fine art collection in the Musée Cheret (or Musée des Beaux Arts), another museum is devoted to Matisse in Cimiez, where he had his studio. There are museums of old Nice, natural history, and the fascinating Palais des Lascaris in the rue Droite, to say nothing of the Musée de la Marine at the foot of the Castle Rock. Nice is a centre for excursions to all the most famous beauty-spots of the Côte d'Azur. There are excursions along the Grande Corniche road, to Eze, St-Jean-Cap-Ferrat, Menton, Monaco, Antibes, the magnificent gorges of the hinterland – to almost all the sites which are practically household names to the holiday-maker.

Cimiez, the health resort of Nice on the top of a hill north of the city, still bears the cachet of Queen Victoria's approval and is still inclined to think of itself as the aristocratic quarter. It has the remains of a Roman amphitheatre which held 6000 spectators, a Villa des Arènes which contains not only the archaeological museum but also the Musée Matisse already mentioned, and a public park, formerly a monastery garden, from which there are good views of Nice. Two other eminences close to Nice which make pleasant short trips are Mont Alban (about 240 metres) and Mont Boron (about 170 metres). These hills mark the eastern "frontier" of Nice, between the Paillon valley and the port of Villefranche.

The Nice Region

Well worth a visit is the hinterland of this last stretch of the Côte d'Azur, the area known as the Nice region. This may be roughly defined as the area limited on the west by a line from Nice to the winter resort of Auron 97 km (60 miles) away, on the north by a line running east-west through St-Etienne-de-Tinee, to the east by a line running from Menton through Sospel and the Vallée de la Vésubie to St-Martin-Vésubie, and on the south by the Mediterranean.

The Nice region is still one of the best places in Europe for a summer holiday with a more dependable proportion of sun than anywhere else – Cannes has an average of about 220 days of sunshine a year; in Menton it is estimated that on average there are no more than 30 really sunless days in the whole year. If some parts of the coast are crowded during the summer peak, the hinterland is rich in mountain villages and small towns where you can still bask in the afternoon sun in the quiet central *place*. Some of the villages are well known, but there are still many for the visitor to discover, a few kilometres either side of the secondary roads. The following suggestions are intended more to put you on the track of your own discoveries than to offer a set programme.

Almost due north from Nice, for example, driving inland for anything between 110 and 150 km (93 miles), depending on detours, there is the valley of the Var, the rocky cleft of the Mescla (37 km (23 miles) from Nice), the hill village of Touet, 55 km (34 miles), with its church built over a mountain stream, Puget-Theniers, 64 km (40 miles), Entrevaux, 71 km (44 miles), the gorges of the Daluis (a diversion from the N202 along the D29), Guillaumes, 97 km (60 miles), with its fine road cut through the rock to the Var, and Valberg, 110 km (69 miles), a winter-sports centre as well as a summer resort. Beyond this point there is another winter-sports centre, Beuil, which is perched on a rock but surrounded by meadows, and the awe-inspiring gorges of the Cians.

A more ambitious run, which gives a comprehensive idea of the attractions of the hinterland, can be made from Nice to Menton by way of Peira Cava and Sospel (roughly 200 km, 124 miles). This would take you from Nice up the Paillon valley (N204) to the vineyards and orchards of Contes, 18 km (11 miles), then on to L'Escarene and up to Luceram, 34 km (21 miles), by the N566, to Peira Cava, 48 km (30 miles), by the D21, and back to N566 and Sospel, 81 km (50 miles). Herè you could make a rewarding diversion (D43) to Fontan, La Brigue and Tende. From Sospel to Menton the Col de Castillon (about 800 metres) gives a view of the Carei river winding down to the sea at Menton.

This naturally suggests the riches of the ımmediate hinterland of Menton itself, with the lovely and still largely unspoilt hill villages of Castellar, Gorbio, St-Agnès and Castillon with their surrounding hills and lush valleys.

Variations on the theme of excursions through the hinterland between Nice and Menton are many and delightful. There are various ways from Cagnes to the gorges of the Verdon. Worth exploring, for example, is the country round St-Martin-Vésubie, the high-altitude resort in the Alpes Maritimes at the foot of the group of mountains which rise to the Argentera (over 305 metres). There is another winter-sports resort nearby at La Colmiane. Another particularly fine drive from Nice goes through the gorges of La Mescla, 37 km (23 miles) by the N202, to La Tour and Clans, and St-Sauveur (N205), and to St-Etienne-de-Tinee, 117 km (73 miles), in the upper valley of the Tinee, which is a summer resort and climbing centre. Then, seven km farther on, is Auron, the most important winter-sports resort of the Southern Alps. If you return to Nice by D39, N205 and N202 the round trip from Nice to Nice will amount to something under 250 km (156 miles).

Back to the coast of coasts, the incomparable Riviera Côte d'Azur. The way east can be taken by the magnificently scenic Grande Corniche (now the A8) which climbs through the foothills by way of La Turbie and Eze, or along the coast road (N7) to the Italian frontier.

Villefranche

If you leave Nice by the old port, driving round its northern end and along the Boulevard Carnot (N559), a six km run round the peninsula of Mount Boron brings you to Villefranche, sheltered between the headland of Nice and Cap Ferrat. Villefranche, with its S.I. in the Jardin François Binon, is still a picturesque fishing port, with a large tourist harbour and a sheltered roadstead deep enough not only for liners and ships on pleasure-cruises, but also for naval vessels, particularly, during the post-war years, United States warships in the Mediterranean.

With something over 6800 inhabitants and about a dozen good hotels, including one four-star establishment, Villefranche is one of the most popular health and holiday resorts, with a shingle beach. The 16th century citadel and fortifications, and the old town, make a pleasant setting, and the poet-painter Jean Cocteau decorated the Chapelle St-Pierre, in the Port de la Santé. Where the *Corniche inférieure* approaches Beaulieu across the neck of Cap Ferrat, the Avenue D. Semeria branches off to take you into the heart of the Cape.

Cap Ferrat

Cap Ferrat, of course, has become best known as one of the favourite resorts of the royal, the rich, and the famous. Leopold II of the Belgians bought the Villa Leopolda, and his son Albert I often stayed there. The villa was later sold to the owner of Fiat. The writer Somerset Maugham lived in the Villa Mauresque, where Winston Churchill was a frequent guest. Fortunately, however, the peninsula is not restricted to the royal, the rich and the renowned: like all the capes along this coast, it gains enormously from the fact that the main coast road goes straight across its neck, leaving the rest of the peninsula luckily deprived of the means of mass entertainment but generously endowed with natural beauty, quiet, and charm. St-Jean (S.I. at 12, Avenue Claude Vigon) has about a dozen hotels (two of them four-star plus – in the "Palace" category), a delightful museum (the Musée Ile-de-France) surrounded by beautiful gardens and built in 1914 by the Baroness Ephrussi de Rothschild on what she once described as "the most beautiful spot in the world", and a zoo. The fishing and holiday village of St-Jean-Cap-Ferrat has 2356 inhabitants, and there are both sandy and shingle beaches. A footpath round the point of the cape gives good views of Beaulieu and Cap d'Ail.

The Promenade Maurice Rouvier links St-Jean with Beaulieu (1.5 km), probably the most sheltered spot along the whole French Mediterranean coast during the winter. (It is one of the places where you will see not only lemon, orange and palm trees but also bananas, although the only fruit I have seen on the stems has looked more decorative than edible.)

Beaulieu, with a two-star S.I. in the Place de la Gare, has a population of 4050, and of its score of hotels two are four-star plus, including the world-famous Réserve de Beaulieu. It is an elegant resort, with a delightful replica of a Greek villa.

Eze

From "Little Africa", the favoured strip of coast between the rocky slopes and the sea where Beaulieu stands, the road brings us to Eze-sur-Mer, a resort with a shingle beach and a pleasant setting that has grown up at the foot of the old village of Eze, perched on a 427-metre rocky eminence.

Eze, with a population of just over 1000 and the S.I. in the Mairie, has ten hotels, including the four-star-plus Cap Esterel. The old village is one of the most picturesque and splendidly situated of all the hill villages close to the coast. There is a tropical garden on a rocky mound, and the village's little museum of local interest should not be missed. In the Chapelle des Penitents Blancs there is a Christ in wood of the Spanish school (1258) of the type you would be more likely to find in Roussillon and the Pyrénées. Mounted over a skull and cross-bones it is known as the Christ of the Black Death and bears an inscription in Catalan which says: 'As you are now, so once was I, and as I am now so shall you be."

Four kilometres east of Eze is Cap d'Ail which, in its small, comparatively secluded and formerly somewhat exclusive way, has retained much of the natural cachet of the wooded capes along this coast. It is an excellent health and bathing resort, with fine beaches shaded by pines. There is much to see in the immediate neighbourhood, nine hotels and a number of camping sites, including the University City Club. From Cap d'Ail eastwards the road, dominated by the Tête de Chien, leads temporarily out of France into the Principality of Monaco.

Monaco

The Principality of Monaco has an astonishing history of 1000-year links with the Grimaldis, which is well worth detailed study under the guidance of the S.I., or rather, as it is styled here, the Direction du Tourisme et des Congrès, at 2A, Boulevard des Moulins, Monte Carlo. The Principality consists of three main focal points: Monaco proper (the Rock) which is the capital; Monte Carlo (which contains the Casino, hotels and shops); and the Condamine, the harbour and sea-level section. There is also an industrial centre, Fontvieille, which has spread westwards towards Cap d'Ail.

The name of Grimaldi first appears as that of a Baron who fought well against the Saracen invaders in the 10th century, but it was in the 13th century that Grimaldis were firmly installed on the Rock. Some of them were allies of the King of France, others acquired domains in Provence. It was, however, Charles I, Admiral of France, Baron of San Demetrio, Lord of Monaco, Roquebrune, Menton and Ventimiglia, who won formal recognition for his extensive holdings. He was, incidentally, wounded at the Battle of Crécy. The Genoese, who had formerly held Monaco, tried to take it back from Charles I's successor, Rainer II, but eventually Genoa had to renounce its claim to Monaco, which became independent under the protection of France and Piedmont-Savoy. There were various changes of allegiance, and after the French Revolution Monaco was attached temporarily to the Alpes-Maritimes Department of France. In 1861, following the war of Italian independence, Charles III of Monaco handed over Roquebrune and Menton to France in return for the withdrawal of French garrisons and a substantial payment. The boundaries then established are those of the Principality today.

The present population is about 24,000, which goes up to 26,000 in the high summer. The size of the Principality is 386 acres (about one-sixtieth of the size of Paris), and the total territory of Monaco is about 3505 metres long and it ranges between 487 and 975 metres in width. Only 4000 of the inhabitants of Monaco have Monégasque citizenship, which exempts them from taxation and military service. Of the permanent population, Monte Carlo and the Condamine have about 10,000 each, the rest live on the Rock.

Today's visitors to this fairy-tale principality who are shocked beyond measure at the skyscraper buildings and other harsh modern developments that disfigure the waterfront may take comfort from the fact that it might have been much worse: the destruction of the natural beauty and grandeur of the site were halted, it is claimed, before it was too late, and everything – it is also claimed – is now under control.

It is true, of course, that it has not been a process of totally uncontrolled development. The removal of the Paris–Ventimiglia surface railway where it passed through Monaco, and its diversion into a 3-km tunnel under the Monte Carlo and Beausoleil hills in 1964, not only healed an ugly scar, but also added something like 50,000 square metres to the available land in the Principality. The creation of beaches, more pleasure-port facilities, underground garages, sea-front promenades, new jetties and a much needed housing complex at Fontvieille represent gains as well as losses, even though the waterfront buildings already tend to destroy the visual character of the natural site and deprive it of its once unique charm.

But the Palace is still the Palace and its operatic glamour is as great a draw to visitors as ever it was. Monte Carlo has fine shops and its streets have a superb mountain backcloth: the Casino is still a triumph of wedding-cake architecture and its terrace is still beautiful. And, apart from its remaining picture-book qualities, its contributions to the arts and the sciences are considerable – including the serious study of the social aims, development and vocabulary of "tourism". Every holidaymaker who has visited Monaco knows of the Botanical Gardens, the Zoological Acclimatisation Centre and the world-famous Oceanographic Museum, under the direction of Commandant Cousteau. Equally well-known among motor racing and sporting enthusiasts is the Monte Carlo Rally and the annual Monaco Grand Prix which, miraculously, uses the winding streets of Monte Carlo as its circuit. This exciting and hair-raising event takes place in May.

The Prince's Palace, begun by the Genoese in 1215, stands in a square that takes up the width of the Rock. Many parts of the Palace and its approaches –except the private gardens on the north-west side – may be visited during the season. A charge is made for admission, with a reduction for children, but children under 10 are admitted free.

The Condamine, which has suffered considerably from the point of view of its scenic charm between the Rock and Monte Carlo, as a result of the proliferation of skyscrapers, is none the less an essential and interesting part of the Monaco complex, not only because it has the Church of Ste-Devote and the Zoological Centre, but also because it is a homely cluster of residential and business streets in which, one feels, the normal life of the Principality goes on, and in which the real Monégasques live and work.

Monte Carlo

Monte Carlo, built on the Plateau des Spélugues, was given its name as recently as 1866, when Prince Charles III of Monaco decided to call it "Mount Charles" in the Italianate version. The Plateau des Spélugues (from the Latin, *spelunca*, "cave") was so-called from the caves at the foot of the Rock, and was originally the property of an hotel proprietor in Monaco. Acquisition of the site was followed by the creation of the "Société des Bains de Mer et du Cercle des Étrangers de Monaco" (S.B.M.) which made Monte Carlo the European capital of games of chance. The S.B.M. has been controlled since 1966 by the State of Monaco.

The interest of most summer visitors today in the Casino and its beautiful surroundings is architectural rather than aleatoric. One of the public rooms, the Salle Garnier, and part at least of the Theatre, were designed by Charles Garnier, architect of the Paris Opéra. It was in this theatre that Diaghilev's Russian Ballet came into being, and many of the older generation today, even if their memories do not go back to Diaghilev, will always associate Monte Carlo with the Ballets Russes de Monte Carlo which did so much to create a real audience for ballet in London. Those, on the other hand, whose interest is primarily in the gaming rooms, need to obtain their tickets for the public or private rooms during the morning.

In a way the most enjoyable part of the whole complex is still Monte Carlo town, with its pleasant streets, elegant shops and superb pastry-cooks. It makes a very agreeable base for an extensive exploration of the area. Monte Carlo Beach, still largely the preserve of a wealthy minority, is in French territory.

In the immediate neighbourhood of Monaco–Monte Carlo is Beausoleil, which was created in 1903 out of part of the territory of La Turbie. In effect it is an extension of the upper part of Monte Carlo, from which it is separated by a symbolic frontier. Beausoleil, with about 14,000 inhabitants (S.I. in the Mairie), is a well-placed small resort with some good hotels and is close to the Mont des Mules, with magnificent views. La Turbie (on the D53 from Beausoleil), with its magnificent Roman remains and its breathtaking views over the coast, is an absolute must: farther east along the Grande Corniche comparable views are available from the Vistaero restaurant, 300 metres above sea-level, and, of course, from other points nearby. Between Monte Carlo and Menton is another pleasant cape, Cap Martin; before going on to Menton leave your car somewhere practical near the N599 and explore Cap Martin on foot. It is part of the joint commune of Roquebrune–Cap Martin, and well worth visiting.

Menton

Menton is still the queen of the Riviera. A modern queen, perhaps, not terribly smart, even a little blowzy, but in complexion, health, confidence and natural superiority, a queen all the same. She was born to be queen: nowhere along the whole Mediterranean coastline of France, from Cerbère to Ventimiglia, are conditions more propitious for a royal birth and a regal life. Senseless, money-grubbing damage is being done all round her and many of her most charming attributes have already been reduced to memories, but while relics of the reign of Menton remain the Riviera will never be entirely lost.

It is a long story. Local legend takes it back to Adam and Eve, for it was Eve who, clutching a lemon to her breast as she and Adam were driven from Eden, made no attempt to plant it until she came to a spot between blue sea and great mountains, where conditions were ideal. This was Menton, where the golden fruit flourishes in the gardens and at the sheltered feet of the Alps.

Fanciful legends apart, man discovered the advantages of living there as long ago as the Palaeolithic and Neolithic eras, as the skeletons of Grimaldi and Cro-Magnon men found in the Red Rock caves on what is now the French–Italian frontier indicate.

These early settlers were followed by a great variety of visitors, temporary and otherwise, ranging from Romans, Saracens, Ligurians, the Grimaldis of Monaco, Queen Victoria of Great Britain, the Empress Elizabeth of Austria, the Empress Eugénie, King Albert of the Belgians, sundry other royalties and a liberal sprinkling of statesmen, writers and artists – all of whom have left their mark and have contributed to the unique quality of this evergeen family holiday resort.

Today Menton (with its modern suburb, Carnolès) has more than 25,000 inhabitants and a most efficient and obliging Syndicat d'Initiative in the Palais d'Europe, Avenue Boyer (near what may be described as "the Carnolès end"). These figures are swollen considerably during the summer season, but not, perhaps, to the rather terrifying extent that prevails in some of the younger, trendier resorts along the coast.

What Menton still has to offer, above all, is a modern West End with everything mass-tourism needs, and, in Old Menton itself, one of the loveliest hill-towns of all, climbing through narrow ways and by an elegant stone stairway to the Church of St Michel and the Chapelle des Pénitents-Blancs – both classical 17th century buildings which partly enclose the *parvis* where the annual chamber-music festival is held in August.

This is an enchanted setting. Two sides consist of the elegant façades of the two churches at right angles to each other, with the *parvis* of St Michel serving as the stage for the orchestra or soloist; the third side consists of the tall houses at the top of the old town, whose windows are filled with townspeople enjoying the concerts, and the fourth side is open to the Mediterranean . . . a fabulous back-cloth to a unique setting. The only drawbacks are so rare as to be hardly worth considering – once in a while the acoustics fall below the level of an enclosed concert hall, and there are occasional intrusive sounds from the alleys of the Old Town surrounding the churches: such sounds as village voices, unguarded footsteps, the occasional cat or dog . . . the normal sounds of living which enhance, rather than interrupt the music. As for the quality of the music (everything except the latest novelty), these are some of the participants over the past 15 years or so: Artur Rubinstein, Igor Oistrakh, Nathan Milstein, I Musici, Glenn Gould, Samson François, the Hungarian Quartet, Stuttgart Chamber Orchestra, Wilhelm Kempf, the Vegh Quartet, Biron Janis, Jean-Pierre Rampal, I Virtuosi di Roma, Christian Ferras, Boris Christoff and many others. And since 1977, the violinist Ivry Gitlis has added his own music festival in Garavan's lovely municipal olive-grove, Le Pian.

Music in such a setting, in an ancient town of such charm, sums up much of the appeal of Menton. The town grew on a gently sloping stretch of coast between the promontory of Cap Martin and the cliffs of La Mortola, and is sheltered by a ring of Alpine peaks ranging from Mount Agel (1097 metres) on the west to Mount Grammont (1378 metres) on the frontier with Italy. Thanks to this protective screen, which also refreshes Menton with the four streams of the Gorbio, the Borrigo, the Carei and the Fossan, the *mistral* is practically unknown in this area, and the vegetation is unusually luxuriant. Menton's value as a health resort is known throughout the world, and although the old town and Garavan have suffered some undesirable changes since the resort's Victorian heyday, and beyond the leisurely Boulevard de Garavan there are now motorways slicing through the mountains to the Italian frontier, with a flurry of brash new hotels on the sea-front and a huge new pleasure port, enough remains of the old flavour still to attract the discriminating holidaymaker.

Within the complex of Carnolès–Menton–Garavan itself there is an abundance of entertainment and interest, cultural, sporting and traditional, with, on the one hand, a municipal casino, gaming rooms, swimming pools and an elaborate promenade, and on the other the museum and Library with its fascinating relics of Menton's long struggles for independence and its French–Italian history, to say nothing of the Hôtel de Ville with its register office (or, more romantically, marriage chamber) decorated by Jean Cocteau. There is the Cocteau Museum in the Bastion of the port and – not to be missed – to the east of Garavan there is Les Colombières, a fantastic Renaissance garden designed by the local poet Ferdinand Bac, with a first-class hotel and swimming pool, marvellous walks amid classical statuary, and some of the finest views of the whole coast.

But the essence of Menton, like the essence of all the old Mediterranean French coast settlements that survive with some of their character intact, is compounded of tree-lined small squares where shopkeepers, local residents, visitors, children, indomitable small buses, café waiters and old villagers can rest in the sun or the shade; cool, narrow alleyways under frequent arches; miraculous markets which are a joy to explore and even greater pleasure to shop in; and ancient villas with Paradisal gardens climbing the slopes to the Boulevard de Garavan.

Those who have known Menton over the years will regret that the pleasant old Hôtel des Anglais is, alas, no more, but there are still quite a few of the older establishments, such as the modest New York, charmingly situated in the Chemin Vallaya, Garavan, and the four-star Colombières, in the fascinating Renaissance gardens of that name off the Boulevard de Garavan. The Napoleon, the Chambord, the Europ, the Parc and the Viking are the leading central hotels, but there are dozens of smaller places in the quiet corners between the beach and the Boulevard de Garavan which are particularly characteristic of Menton, such as the Villa Louise, in the Chemin Vallaya.

Apart from the many advantages of Menton itself as a holiday centre its immediate hinterland and surroundings are still, if not entirely unspoilt everywhere (road and apartment-block building are the biggest threats), definitely un-trendy.

Around Menton

Immediately inland from Menton are the mountain villages of Castellar, Castillon, St-Agnès, Gorbio and many others, all accessible by car, local bus, or on foot, each with its own character and charm, and each a splendid centre for wanderings on foot through a lovely countryside. Take, for example, the track from Gorbio to Roquebrune, an easy, winding way, all on about the same contour line, so that when you reach the château of Roquebrune the easy way is then down to the sea road to get the bus back to Menton. The café in the square at Gorbio, incidentally, has a terrace overlooking an extraordinarily lush wooded valley – something of an oasis among the less richly endowed slopes.

These are but a few of the local excursions: there are also delightful trips to be made to Cap Martin–Roquebrune, to Monte Carlo and Monaco, the valleys of the Borrigo and the Castagnins, the Carei valley and, more ambitiously but with abundant reward, as far as Castillon, Sospel, Tende and Brigue.

Index